Warman's

Beatles

FIELD GUIDE

Tim Neely

Values and Identification

©2005 KP Books

Published by

kp books
An Imprint of F+W Publications

700 East State Street • Iola, WI 54990-0001
715-445-2214 • 888-457-2873

Our toll-free number to place an order or obtain
a free catalog is (800) 258-0929.

Library of Congress Catalog Number: 2004115473

ISBN: 0-89689-139-9

Designed by Wendy Wendt

Edited by Tim Neely

Printed in United States of America

Table of Contents

Introduction 4

Why the Beatles Still Matter 8

Ranking the Beatles' Music 15

Memorabilia 33

How to Use This Record Guide 95

Grading Guide 96

Singles 98

7-Inch Extended Plays 249

Albums 272

British Singles in Brief 404

British EPs in Brief 411

British Albums in Brief 417

Label Variations 431

Ex-Beatlemania 457

Conspicuous By Their Absence 469

Together When We're Apart 479

Acknowledgments 502

Index 504

Introduction

The book you are now holding – *Warman's Beatles Field Guide* – is the first of its kind.

Not only does it contain virtually every Beatles group record released by a legitimate American record company, but it also has over 300 photos in full color – all in a book you can carry with you and even stick in your pocket.

Never before has it been so easy to keep track of your Beatles record collection.

Interest in the Beatles remains strong. Prices for pristine copies of original singles, albums and picture sleeves continue to rise, with no sign of a letup. Other memorabilia – everything from a Shea Stadium poster to Beatles talcum powder – is setting record prices at auction.

Better yet, every new generation of music listeners re-discovers the Beatles; in the first five years of the 2000s, tens of millions of Beatles compact discs have sold – not bad for a band that officially broke up in 1970!

The focus in the *Warman's Beatles Field Guide* is on the records, and most particularly, the seemingly endless variety of releases in the United States. The Beatles didn't truly become a worldwide phenomenon until they began having huge hit records – and causing mass hysteria – in the States. With half a dozen labels cranking out "new" records almost weekly in 1964, it's a challenge to get copies of all of them.

Beatles Essentials

Singles

"She Loves You"
"I Want To Hold Your Hand"
"I Saw Her Standing There"
"A Hard Day's Night"
"Eleanor Rigby"
"Strawberry Fields Forever"

Albums

Rubber Soul
*Sgt. Pepper's Lonely Hearts Club
Band*
White Album
Revolver
Abbey Road

was suddenly of full importance in the sound, instead of just adding his trills, frills and solos. "Day Tripper" was along the same lines, but like the Borg on "Star Trek: The Next Generation," they'd assimilated this new element into the whole so it fit seamlessly, rather than stood out.

Of course, this jumps over the wonderful "Help!"—more Lennon does Dylan, the relatively lightweight "Eight Days A Week," and the god awful "Yesterday." It might have been covered more than any song in history, but that doesn't make "Yesterday" a great song—merely that it appeals to the lowest common denominator of emotions. It's maudlin, a sort of very early dry run for the far more accomplished "Eleanor Rigby." If history was rewritten, and it suddenly vanished forever from human consciousness, Paul would be poorer, but the rest of us would be much better off.

However, it's part of the course that leads up to June 1966. From there until November 1967, one can only surmise the Beatles were working on another plane altogether. There was more space between the releases, allowing them to be more creative. They were using the studio as another instrument, thanks to the capabilities and open mind of George Martin and his engineers. And, obviously, their Muse wasn't taking any holidays. How else do you explain "Paperback Writer" b/w "Rain," "Penny Lane" b/w "Strawberry Fields Forever," "All You Need Is Love" b/w "Baby You're A Rich Man," and "Hello Goodbye" b/w "I Am The

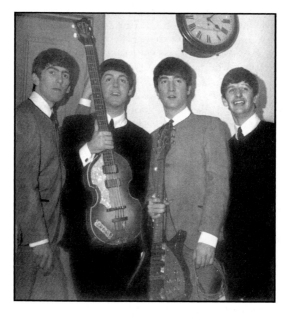

Walrus." Yes, there were a couple of other singles in there, too, but they were filler (as was "Hello Goodbye," really). In 17 months, this group expanded the whole definition of pop music, adding levels of complexity that still resonate— notably when a group is described as "Beatlesque" these days, it's this period the word evokes.

While they'd been edging away from the standard form of the pop song, the blueprint that had been laid down years before (as had Dylan, although he came to it from folk, bringing in a completely different, and far more socially conscious, element), it wasn't until "Paperback Writer" that

they'd made the jump. *Rubber Soul,* their first real album, a disc that was a whole in feel and execution rather than a collection of tracks, had been the first step in the direction, and *Revolver* was the giant leap. But "Paperback Writer" and "Rain" told us what was happening. They were disturbing, not comforting as pop music had always been. They weren't love songs. In fact, at the time, you'd have been hard pressed to really understand the subject matter of the "A" side.

"Paperback Writer" pointed rock in a whole new direction, one which others would pick up on soon enough, while "Rain" was intriguing for its comments on England and sonically for its use of the new possibilities of the studio. And it's worth mentioning that they were superb songs; Lennon and McCartney now had enough confidence in themselves to really let go, and stopping touring would give them the time and freedom to experiment further.

While some of the results of that are songs like "Yellow Submarine" b/w "Eleanor Rigby," there was much stronger fruit, like the precursor to *Sgt. Pepper's Lonely Hearts Club Band,* "Penny Lane" b/w "Strawberry Fields Forever." While "Penny Lane" seems conventional (as do all Paul's songs, really), it's McCartney pushing his own envelope in a lyrical masterpiece, a wonderful sketch of a place, while the arrangement evokes the very British institution of a Salvation Army band.

But it's the other side where the Beatles reach their musical zenith. If John Lennon had only written "Strawberry Fields Forever" it would be enough to qualify him for genius status, even if it's really two songs. Full credit to George Martin, too, but ultimately it's about the Beatles themselves—just listen to *Anthology* for the way the song develops through the process of trial and error. Maybe none of them knew exactly what they were groping for, but they understood when they'd found it.

From there, "All You Need Is Love" actually pulls back a little, a knock-off full of self-reverential humor. But it's still light years ahead of the singles other groups were releasing. It was certainly more than "just" a single. The theme was ideal for the summer of love, and that live broadcast between 21 countries (although it was deflating to understand the track wasn't being recorded live for the 45 which appeared in shops the following Friday).

It's the flip that makes it something special, with George's "Baby You're A Rich Man," one of the most accessible of the Indian-flavored songs, and one of the best, with a recognizable, even singable chorus. No one had put a song like that on a single before—but they soon would. It might not have been a musical high point for the Beatles, or even for George, but it showed they were still looking around, still breaking down barriers, if only because they didn't see the barriers there in the first place. In this brave new world, anything was possible.

And it was. "Hello Goodbye" might have been a throwaway, but the flip side, taken from *Magical Mystery Tour,* was "Strawberry Fields" taken five or six stops down the line. "I Am The Walrus" was archetypal Lennon, with its clever wordplay, and some very disturbing, graphic images. And by utilizing the electric piano as the main instrument, it put the group in a very different place. Soaked in psychedelia, yes, but also something that stands completely alone, in many ways apart from the Beatles canon as a twisted, but beautiful, piece of music.

Like any good run, it had to come to an end, however. And when they re-emerged with "Lady Madonna" in March 1968, it was apparent that they'd moved back, which would be reflected in the Beatles later that year. "Lady Madonna" was McCartney's tribute to Fats Domino, but why? Fats was still around, and capable of doing that piano thing much better than Paul ever could. It was a fun little party piece, but that was all, and certainly not worthy of release, which can also be said for "Hey Jude," which was, at best, half a song and an ending that lasted forever. Even "Revolution" didn't exactly storm the musical barricades, based on the kind of 12-bar structure they'd all played forever. So, after the daring adventures of '67 came the retreat of '68 (the same thing that would lead the Band into Music from Big Pink), and the end of good Beatles singles. "Get Back"? Nice little live number, but not worth the vinyl. "Something"? Great song. Wonderful George Harrison single. But it's not really the Beatles, is it? It even seems out of place on the nearly perfect album *Abbey Road*. "Let It Be"? Put it on McCartney and it would have been perfectly at home. "The Long And Winding Road"? An embarrassment to all concerned.

Which makes a total of six essential, need-to-be-in-every-record-collection singles ("She Loves You," "I Want to Hold Your Hand," "I Saw Her Standing There," "A Hard Day's Night," "Eleanor Rigby" and "Strawberry Fields Forever"). Harsh, you say? Not by the standards the Beatles unconsciously set themselves. And it's six more than most bands ever manage. The best singles were more than songs, they were mini-albums, rich in content, far beyond the three- or four-chord trick that had started the decade (and the band's career). They'd brought us to a complexity undreamed of in 1960, and given a depth to popular music.

And while they did make a few glorious singles, their achievements lie more in their albums. To be fair, their first few LPs followed the mold, a big song or two, plenty of covers, and a few of their own songs. They were haphazard collections. Even the two movie soundtracks, which had some cohesion by virtue of their association with the films, weren't really albums.

That had to wait until *Rubber Soul,* where the influence of Bob Dylan is on every single track. But, like everything else they took on board, it's distilled into something else that could only be the Beatles—by then they were so assured in what they were doing that it couldn't be any other way.

Even then, it's hardly a concept album, but one unified in feel. It wasn't preceded by a single, so there was no "hook" on which to peg it—not that they needed one by December 1965. The acoustic guitar ran through all the tracks like an underpinning, and while the songs tended to work within the standard verse/chorus/verse/chorus/bridge/solo/verse/chorus framework that had long typified pop music, they added elements, like the sitar on "Norwegian Wood." Much of the

lyrical content moved beyond the boy-girl idea of romance
on tracks like "Nowhere Man," "Think For Yourself" and
"Norwegian Wood," that wonderfully veiled confession of
infidelity.

If you like, *Rubber Soul* was the first real LP that could
stand (or fall) as a single entity. It's remarkable, however,
that just nine months after they could have taken a further
quantum leap with *Revolver*, parts of which put them out
beyond the stratosphere, on tracks like "Tomorrow Never
Knows" and "And Your Bird Can Sing," two of the most

adventurous pieces ever released on vinyl—and really only released because of who the artists were. Of course, they were tempered by songs like "Taxman," "Got To Get You Into My Life," "Yellow Submarine" and "Here, There And Everywhere," which offered an anchor in the familiar before casting off. But all the songs had an otherworldly dreaminess, even the singalong "Yellow Submarine," to let everything hang together in a psychedelic space. LSD hung all over it, but it would over so much music in another year or so. As usual, the Beatles weren't just ahead of the curve, they were the curve.

It would take them a year to come up with *Sgt. Pepper's Lonely Hearts Club Band,* probably the most influential album of the rock era, and one where, for the first time, the general public came to see the possibilities of the album form.

Whether or not it was really a concept album is irrelevant. Songs like "Lucy In The Sky With Diamonds," "She's Leaving Home," and, of course, "A Day In The Life" moved so far beyond the pop experience that they could only exist as part of an LP, rather than on their own as singles where, frankly, no one would have known what to make of them anyway. They were buzzing along light years ahead of the public.

Really, *Sgt. Pepper* proved that the album was the only form big enough for their creativity, even though it scared them—hence the return to the idea of basics on the *White*

Album, which was presaged by the throwaway pastiche of "Lady Madonna."

But for all the Beatles tried to get back to a more innocent state, they'd come too far, too fast, and couldn't find their way home. "Helter Skelter" wasn't just rock 'n' roll, it was a primal scream of the lost, while "Dear Prudence" and "Glass Onion" were "Lucy In The Sky With Diamonds" taken three steps further. There was very little basic about the album at all. It sprawled wildly, and for once they made no attempt to stop it—it was as if they were seeing just how far they could go, not editing, pouring everything out. For all that it splayed all over the place, it was an album, as if they'd lost the ability to think in terms of singles any more, which they had. They'd become used to working on larger canvases, and after the ceiling of the Sistine Chapel, who wanted to go back to a postcard?

If it all came together in one perfect shining moment, that was *Abbey Road.* Everything they'd learned came into play here, from the playful psychedelia of "Come Together"—Chuck Berry recast as a hippie—to George's guitar workout, showing his mastery of so many styles (including that "Woman" tone, a reference to Eric Clapton). The "suite" that fills most of side two is a work of genius, the songs segueing smoothly one to the next as if they'd been designed that way. It could only have worked on an album, and one with a daring conception. Then the cheeky afterthought of "Her Majesty" rounded things off in a smiling manner. They might be cultural world leaders, but somewhere underneath the Scouse mop tops still lurked.

There was still the small matter, and it was a small matter, of *Let It Be,* conceived and executed in acrimony and with songs scarcely worthy the name by any standards, let alone those established by the Beatles. But it's better forgotten, a product of rancor that should never have seen the light of day.

And so the Beatles leave six great singles and five great albums. Maybe that doesn't seem like too much, not enough to support the legend. But, really, those are the records that made the legend. Not that the rest is filler, but these are in a different class. They're inspired, and that much inspiration is rare in any career, let alone one that only lasted eight years. The intensity and speed with which they worked was incredible, and unthinkable by today's standards, where two years between albums is the norm.

But they were different times, when anything was possible, and everything the Beatles achieved was new. They blazed so many trails, left so many markers, that music is still struggling to catch up. They led us by the hand from childhood to what was, at least, adolescence. And in those tracks, those singles and albums, they gave us nirvana.

Memorabilia

Just about any non-recorded memorabilia associated with the Beatles is collectible.

Over the years, literally hundreds of books and magazines have been dedicated to some aspect of the Fab Four. Many licensed products, from the sublime to the ridiculous, were made available, and almost all are highly sought.

In the next pages, we have illustrated some selected products relating to the Beatles, most of which were made available for sale to the public, and some prices these items might fetch, depending on condition. *This is a representative selection, not an exhaustive one.*

Most of the interest in memorabilia falls under several categories:

- Posters, tickets, programs and other material relating to the Beatles in concert.
- Officially licensed material from the height of Beatlemania (1964 especially).
- Material relating to the Beatles in their movies, with special emphasis on the many Yellow Submarine products.

Unless the item was extremely nice or extremely limited, Beatles items from the years after they broke up (1970 forward), though still interesting, are not as sought-after as the material from the early years.

The observant reader will see that a few of the price ranges for memorabilia are wider than those found in the records section. This is because we've chosen to quote values for copies in **very good** (lower part of the range) to **near mint** (upper part of the range) condition. With some of these items, truly near-mint examples are not known to exist, thus a VG item might be the only way to obtain an item in presentable condition. "Very good" doesn't mean "trashed"; it is still presentable, but has noticeable defects.

Beware of Forgeries!

Because of the growing market, many Beatles items have been counterfeited. Your best bet, when paying a lot for a piece of Beatles history, is to buy from a trusted dealer or auction house, especially one with a specialty in the Beatles or rock 'n' roll in general.

A Special Note About Autographs

Signatures of the four Beatles, especially all on the same item, are extremely collectible. They are also extremely rare, as after 1963, the group had relatively little contact with the public in situations where a fan might get an autograph.

Obviously, the best way to obtain any autograph is to do it in person. Alas, with John Lennon and George Harrison, this is no longer possible.

The next best way is to get it from a reputable dealer. But forgeries and "honest fakes" abound: It's been said that at least 75 percent of all the Beatles autographs for sale on popular Internet auction sites are not authentic.

"Honest fakes" were done by people close to the Beatles, usually Neil Aspinall, their road manager, or others in their publicity department, to fulfill the thousands of requests for autographs. They were not done with malicious intent – but they also are not genuine Beatles signatures and don't fetch as much as the Fabs' actual signatures.

The best advice before spending big money on a Beatles autograph is check with an expert. Fortunately, in recent years Frank Caiazzo has come to the rescue. He is the world's top authority on Beatles autographs, and any piece he has authenticated is as close to guaranteed as humanly possible. (But beware; some unscrupulous sellers have actually forged his certificate of authenticity!) To learn more about Caiazzo and his services, visit his Web Site (www.beatlesautographs. com).

Autographed Album. "Sgt. Pepper's Lonely Hearts Club Band" album opened to the color photos of the group and signed by each member above their heads, includes special presentation inscription, ca. late 1967, overall 21 3/4" x 24"…**$57,500.**

Autographed Album. "Please Please Me" album cover signed by the Beatles with Jimmie Nicol, who filled in for drummer Ringo Starr on a June 1964 tour of several countries, signatures are light, water staining to back cover, very rare, very good condition...**$8,000+.**

Autographs. Signed in blue ballpoint pen on a pink piece of paper, matted with a color-tinted photograph of the group, ca. 1963, overall 17 3/4" x 21 3/4"...**$2,585.**

Autographs: A complete set of Beatles autographs on
an album page, light green in color, John Lennon and
George Harrison signed in blue ballpoint, Paul McCartney
and Ringo Starr signed in green ballpoint with McCartney
adding "The Beatles," early 1963...**$6,500+.**

Baseball. Signed by John Lennon...**$1,700+**

Bobb'n Head Dolls. Long before the "bobblehead dolls" craze of the late 1990s, Car Mascot made this package of the Beatles as "Bobb'n Head" dolls in 1964. Original editions are 8" tall and came in a custom package with cardboard on either side of each head to keep the heads from moving; reproductions are often smaller and are less detailed than the authentic version … **All 4 figures, still in box: $700 - $1,400.**

Bobb'n Head Dolls. Beatles figures, each on square base with name written on front, wearing matching green Nehru jackets and trousers, bowl-cut hair, playing guitars and drum, near mint condition, ca. 1964, set…**$1,225.**

Bubble Bath. Colgate made these "Soakies" in 1965. Only Paul and Ringo versions were made; their heads screwed off to remove the liquid from inside. These can go for more if there is still bubble bath inside… **Paul version $60 - $120; Ringo version: $50 - $100.**

Calendar: Salesman's sample with "Your Imprint Here" information, 1964, sturdy cardboard, factory folded in middle, very good condition, 24" x 38"…**$200+.**

Calendar: "Make a date with the Beatles" with moveable day, date and month, U.K., 1964…**$100+.**

Cartoon Cel. Tile cel from 1966 Beatles animated weekly cartoon series, shows the four band members with facsimile signatures, three-layer, excellent condition, framed, 10" x 13 1/2" (some tape on edges)…**$3,061.**

Cartoon Kit. Colorforms product says, "Yeah! Yeah! Yeah! Here are all four Beatles now in Colorforms Plastic," 1966…**$50-$100.**

Coloring Book. Beatles, Saalfield, 1964…**$50-$100.**

Comic Books. The world of superheroes noticed the Beatles as well. From September 1964, here's an edition of *Superman's Pal Jimmy Olson* (DC Comics) with a story about Jimmy becoming a Beatles-like teen idol … **$6.25 - $25.**

Compact. Goldtone, round, the lid decorated with picture of the Beatles, unmarked, rare… **$475.**

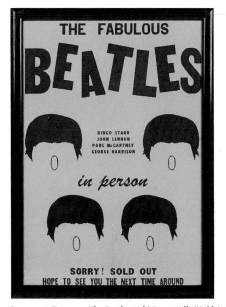

Concert Poster. The Beatles 1964 Forest Hills "Sold Out" poster, thought to be the only one to ever appear in the marketplace, posted after all tickets were sold for Aug. 28-29 concerts at Forest Hills Tennis Stadium, dry-mounted, intersections of folds show wear, seven small holes, 28 1/2" x 40"…**$9,500.**

Concert Poster. The Beatles concert at New York's Shea
Stadium on Aug. 23, 1966, one of four posters known,
produced by Murray Poster Printing Co., excellent condition
with minor creases, 18" x 23 1/2"…**$15,000.**

Concert Poster. The Beatles played at Cleveland Stadium on Aug. 14, 1966, one of three posters known, produced by Jontzen Printers, set of staple holes in each corner, lightly wrinkled, psychedelic design in pencil on reverse, 14 1/2" x 20"…**$15,000.**

Concert Program. "The Beatles Show," British publication with photos and biographical information on the band, includes a 6" x 8" photo from the press kit mailed with the program, 1963, 16 pages, excellent condition…**$230.**

Concert Ticket. Beatles concert ticket, full ticket for Aug. 20, 1965, concert at White Sox Park, Chicago, lavender with black printing, near mint…**$827.**

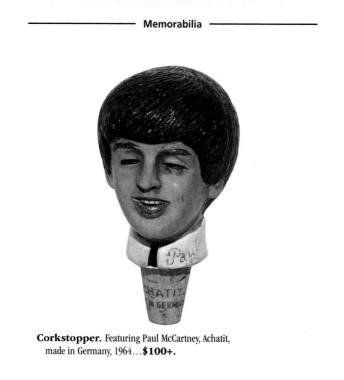

Corkstopper. Featuring Paul McCartney, Achatit,
made in Germany, 1964…**$100+.**

Dolls. Vinyl with large head and rooted hair, any of the four, with instruments, Remco, each...**$100-$250.**

Dress. White cotton, sleeveless, knee-length with horizontal yellow thin and wide stripes, and printed with various Beatles-related images in blue and black, including words and music of their songs, the Beatles' faces and signatures, ca. 1960s...**$460.**

"**Flip Your Wig**" **Game.** Made by Milton Bradley, this
game is more common than most people think, but it's
one of the more sought-after items from Beatlemania. As
with all older games, it's tough to find with everything
intact and a solid box ... **$50 - $100.**

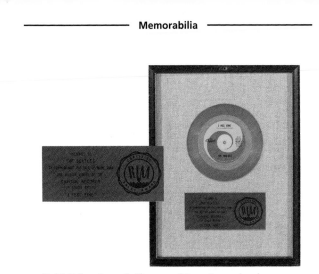

Gold Sales Award. Plaque on white matte award reads:
"Presented To The Beatles To Commemorate The Sale Of More
Than One Million Copies Of The Capitol Records Pop Single
Record 'I Feel Fine,'" 1964, 13 1/4" x 17 1/4"…**$4,000+.**

Guitars. Several different Beatles-related toy guitars were issued, both in the United States and England. This one was made by Selcol in England ... **$250 – $500.**

Hair Spray. What better to keep one's Beatle hairdo in place
than spray with the Beatles' own images on it? Made by Bronson
Products in 1964, this has been counterfeited by putting color
photocopies on another can of spray. Most surviving cans
show signs of their age, such as label tears and rust; if it looks
too good to be true, it probably is … **$200 - $600.**

Halloween Costume. Made for all four Beatles by Ben Cooper
Inc. in Brooklyn, N.Y., these tended to be worn, and are rarely seen
still in their original boxes… **Ringo costume: $100-$300.**

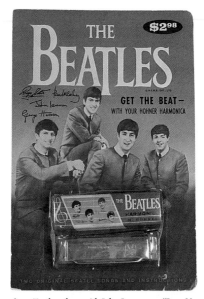

Harmonica. To play along with John Lennon on "Love Me Do" or "Please Please Me," why not use an official Hohner Beatles harmonica? The harmonica itself is generic; the outer box makes it worthwhile. It also came in a blister pack attached to a fold-open songbook with two songs inside. In the 1960s, this sold for $2.98. Complete set ... **$600 - $1,200.**

Jacket. Midshipman-style jacket of blue-grey wool, black
   label on inside pocket says "Jacob Reed And Sons…Fine
   Uniforms…Since 1824," signed by George Harrison
   on left breast with black marker…**$800+.**

John Lennon Album. Autographed album "Imagine,"
   signed and inscribed in blue ballpoint pen on the front
   cover, "To Sheryl love John Lennon 76," with a self-portrait
   caricature of Lennon's smiling face, additionally annotated
   at lower right corner with a doodle of a couple looking up at
   a four-legged animal standing on a cloud…**$8,050.**

John Lennon's Spectacles. Wire-rimmed, prescription
   lenses, matted in a shadowbox frame with a color machine print
   photograph of Lennon wearing a similar pair, accompanied by a letter
   concerning the provenance, overall 11 1/2" x 16 1/2"…**$25,875.**

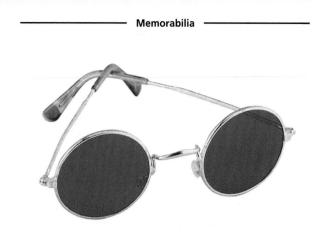

John Lennon's Sunglasses. Blue-tinted glasses
personally owned by Lennon were given to a friend by his
Uncle Charlie in August 1994 at the Cavern Club Tour
Concert, comes with photos of the event…**$1,000+.**

John Lennon and Yoko Ono. Recording, one-sided acetate of
"Sunday, Bloody Sunday," 45 rpm, with "The Master Cutting Room"
white label with typed details, dated "2/24/72," inscribed by Lennon
at the bottom, accompanying sleeve also inscribed, matted with color
machine print photo of Lennon, overall 15" x 24"…**$1,092.**

Kaboodle Kit. Could be used as a lunchbox,
Standard Plastics Products Inc., 1964…**$350+.**

Lamp. Made in England, this desk lamp has a fragile shade, 7" in diameter, plus a black base. Sometimes the shade is found without the base, and vice versa, but for the entire thing … **$600 - $1,500.**

Lunch Box. Metal with thermos bottle, Aladdin, 1966...**$800.**

Lunch Box. Metal, marked "Aladdin Industries Incorporated,
Nashville, Tenn. Copyright 1965 NEMS Enterprises, Ltd.," scratches
and soiling, no thermos, 8" wide, 3 3/4" deep, 7" high...**$259.**

Magic Card Trick. Unusual item sold through mail order or in magic shops, features heavy cardboard cards, 7" x 9" of the Beatles, real beetles and a girl, comes in paper sleeve shaped like a TV set with four pages of instructions, made by Supreme Magic Co., Devon, U.K... **$600+.**

Model Kit. John, Paul, George or Ringo, Revell, plastic kits, 1965, each .... **$75-$225.**

Mug: Porcelain, slightly tapering cylindrical shape
with C-form handle, marked in back "The Beatles"
with portraits and names in black on white, "England"
stamped on bottom, ca. 1963, 4" high…**$230.**

Mug Set. Royal Doulton set of four Beatles from Sgt. Pepper era, 1984, plus extra special edition John Lennon mug from 1987, hand painted and highly detailed, made in U.K., mint, 4" x 5" x 6"...**$500+.**

Oil Paint Sets. Each of the Beatles was the subject of one of these boxes, manufactured by Artistic Creations, Inc. This is for unpainted examples still in the box with the paints and brush intact… **John Lennon version: $400-$1,200; Paul McCartney version: $150-$600.**

Oil Paint Sets. Manufactured by Artistic Creations, Inc. This is for unpainted examples still in the box with the paints and brush intact... **George Harrison version: $125 - $500; Ringo Starr version: $125 -$500.**

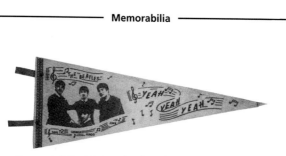

Pennant. With original tassels and metal grommets, depicts Beatles with "Yeah, Yeah, Yeah" slogan, white, red and blue, Canada, ca. 1964, 21"
.... **$383.**

Photograph. Autographed publicity shot of the Beatles, signed on front in blue ink by all four members of the group, matted, 1963, 8" x 10"
.... **$5,175.**

Pillow. Caricatures and facsimile signatures of the
Beatles, made by Nordic House, 1964... **$100+.**

Portraits. Painted by Nicholas Volpe, then mass-produced by NEMS/Seltaeb, these attractive 14x18 prints suitable for framing are a popular collectible. Original editions have printing at the lower right corner of the portraits... **Set of all 4, $50 - $100.**

Posters, movie. Movie posters, or "one-sheets," as they are known, are hot collectibles, and the Beatles' four movie posters – *A Hard Day's Night; Help!; Yellow Submarine;* and *Let It Be* – are among the hottest. Beware, because reprints exist of most of the sought-after titles...**Yellow Submarine one-sheet: $200 - $400.**

Poster. "A Hard Day's Night," United Artists, 1964, shows partial photo of each of the Beatles, white background, blue, red and black lettering, three-sheet, 41" x 81"...**$1,763.**

Poster. "Yellow Submarine," United Artists, 1968, three-sheet, illustrations of characters from the film in vibrant colors, "Nothing is real" in red at the top, with red-rimmed black box in center containing a drawing of a yellow submarine and "The Beatles – Yellow Submarine" in orange-shadowed yellow type, linen backed, 41" x 81"...**$2,115.**

Promotional Display. Easel-backed display for the "Beatles '65" album, rare, considerable damage including bent corners, nicks, water stains, 21 3/4" x 21 3/4"…**$1,000+.**

Promotional Drum Display. Titanic vintage drum was a
store display for "Sgt. Pepper's Lonely Hearts Club Band" album,
1967, plexiglass drum head hand-lettered with tin rim, built-in light
fixture, 36" in diameter, 8 1/2" deep, very good condition…**$300+.**

Promotional LP Flat. "Beatles For Sale" U.K.
store display flat, "Printed in England," 1964, rare,
excellent condition, 12 1/4" square...**$300+**

Promotional Poster. Capitol Records promo poster for "Twist & Shout," called "The Hit Single," very rare, some creases and edge wear, 12" x 36"…**$400+.**

Promotional Poster. The Beatles' "White Album" poster announces "It's Here!" in 3 1/2" red lettering along top border, minor wrinkling at corners, small tear at top border, 23" x 38"…**$300+.**

Record Cases (Regular). Manufactured under license from NEMS by Air Flite in 1964, these are both an LP carrying case and a 45 rpm carrying case ... **LP case: $150 - $500; 45 case: $100 - $300.**

Record Cases (Disk-Go). Charter Industries made seven
different colors of these 45 rpm carrying cases, with the twist-off top
and the spindle in the middle. Manufactured in 1966, counterfeits
exist, but the fakes don't have the faces and lettering embedded in
the plastic. Brown cases are the rarest. Each … **$100 - $300.**

Record Player. One of the rarest of all commercially available Beatles items is this portable four-speed record player. It came in a carrying case, which sometimes can be found without the record player inside. Only 5,000 were made; these sold for $29.99 in 1964, but they go for a lot more today ... **$3,000 - $10,000.**

Ringo Starr's Drumsticks: Pair of drumsticks owned and used by Beatles' drummer, 1960s, embossed "arbiter...Ringo Starr...model...Made In England...Hickory," well-used...**$3,000+.**

Snare Drum. Just as there were toy Beatles guitars, so there were toy Beatles (or more specifically, Ringo) drums. This version, made by Selcol in the U.K., has his face on the drum head … **$400 - $1,200.**

Tie-tack set. The Beatles with each tack featuring the likeness of a Beatle, base metal, silver color, original card, ca. 1965, four pieces, set…**$150.**

Talcum Powder. Made by Margo of Mayfair in England, this
is one of the toughest items to find, and it's especially tough to
find cans that aren't rusty or dented … **$400 - $800.**

Three-Ring Binders. Many kids carried their love of the Beatles with them in school with these attractive items, which were popular in 1964 and 1965. Two different companies made them in eight different colors; white binders made by New York Looseleaf are the most common, other colors made by Standard Plastic Products less so … **White binder, $100 - $200; other colors, $150 - $400.**

Tickets. Ticket stubs, and especially unused tickets, for any Beatles-related event from the 1960s are sought-after souvenirs. Stubs bring a fraction of the price of an unused ticket, but for some concerts, there are still no known examples of unused tickets! Reproductions exist of most of the key tickets, so be careful. These are unused tickets from the 1965 Shea Stadium, New York, concert, very few of which are known to exist … **$2,000 - $6,000.**

The 1966 Candlestick Park concert was the Beatles' last paid concert. More unused tickets from this concert exist than most, as it was not a sellout ... **$200 – $600.**

Wristwatch. Even today, there are licensed Beatles watches. But this is a vintage women's watch made by Bradley with Beatles heads at 12, 3, 6 and 9 o'clock; it's sought after by Bradley watch collectors as well as Fab Four enthusiasts … **$400 - $1,000.**

Yellow Submarine Action Figure. Beatles with accessories, McFarlane, 1999, 8" high, each…**$6-$12.**

Yellow Submarine Banks. Made by Pride Creations in 1968, the best copies still have the "King Features Subafilms" stickers on the bottom and the rubber stoppers ....**Set of 4, $375. - $1,500.**

Yellow Submarine Bicycle. Lady's model, Huffy, three-speed, yellow painted frame, seat decorated with printed design featuring the submarine, bases on the Beatles movie, ca. late 1960s......... **$2,500.**

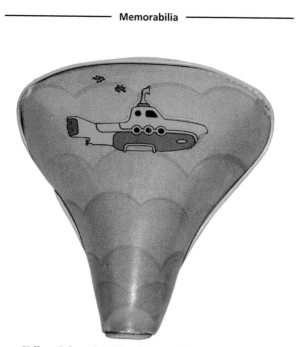

Yellow Submarine Bicycle Seat. Made
by Huffy, 1968, decorated with printed design of the
submarine, very good condition...**$500+.**

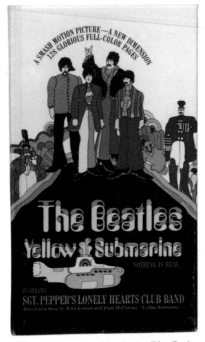

Yellow Submarine Book. Small hardback
book, World Publishing, 1968…**$50.**

Yellow Submarine Clock. Alarm clock,
made by Sheffield, 1968…**$75.**

Yellow Submarine Lunchbox. From 1968,
complete with the Thermos bottle ... **$100 - $400.**

Yellow Submarine Photo Album. Snapshot
album by A & M Leatherline, 1968...**$50+.**

Yellow Submarine Puzzles. Jaymar made 19 different *Yellow Submarine* jigsaw puzzles in 1968, in large, medium and small or "pocket" sizes. The large ones, in 12x12 boxes, are most collectible, but the other sizes are sought, too. The price assumes the box is intact and all the pieces are there .... **Medium puzzle, $80 - $150 each.**

Yellow Submarine Toy. Die cast toy submarine,
by Corgi Toys, in original box, 1968…**$200+.**

Yellow Submarine Watercolor Set. Paint set
with four 6" x 8" "Swing'n Pictures" and six "Groovy
nontoxic colors," Craft Master, 1968…**$200+.**

How to Use This Record Guide

This section of this book is divided into three parts:

- ■ Singles
- ■ 7-inch extended play singles
- ■ Albums

The singles are listed in alphabetical order by the title of the bigger hit side. In some cases where different editions of the same record declared a different A-side than the bigger hit, they are cross-referenced. For example, look up "Strawberry Fields Forever" in the listings and you'll be referred to the listings under "Penny Lane." The EPs and albums are listed alphabetically by the title.

Under each title we have listed the label and number and all the known variations, pretty much in the order they were available. Spelled out in detail is how to distinguish the different versions.

Finally, we list a range of values for copies in top-notch collectible condition. We have defined this as Very Good Plus at worst to Near Mint at best. Most Beatles records from the 1960s are lucky to meet the low end of this standard, much less the high end.

The prices are meant to be averages rather than maximums, although in some cases, they may be maximums. Some trusted dealers can, and will, sell items for more than the prices listed. They aren't trying to rip you off – you are also buying some of the trust and reputation that comes from dealing with them. Also, if you plan to sell your Beatles material, remember that if you are selling to a dealer, you will get a fraction of the quoted prices.

Grading Guide

Condition means everything – and this is even truer
with Beatles material than most others, as many of the
singles and LPs listed here are actually quite common.
Finding them in top condition is not common.

Remember, the price range in this book is for **very
good to near mint condition.**

MINT (M)

These are absolutely perfect in every way. Often rumored but
rarely seen, Mint should never be used as a grade unless more
than one person agrees that the record truly is in this condition.

NEAR MINT (NM OR M–)

A good description of a NM record is "it looks like it just came from
a retail store and was opened for the first time." In other words, it's
nearly perfect. Many dealers won't use a grade higher than this,
implying (perhaps correctly) that no record is ever truly perfect.

NM covers should have no creases, folds, seam splits or any
signs of human handling. A near-mint cover also should have no
cutout markings of any kind. It also will have no ring wear.

NM picture sleeves should have no creasing,
ring wear or seam splits of any kind. It should
look as if it has never housed a record.

NM records are shiny, with no visible defects. Writing, stickers
or other markings cannot appear on the label, nor can any

"spindle marks" from someone trying to blindly put the record on the turntable. Major factory defects also must not be present; a record and label obviously pressed off center is not Near Mint.

VERY GOOD PLUS (VG+) OR EXCELLENT (E)

A good description of a VG+ record is "except for a couple minor things, this would be near mint." Most collectors and people who want to play their records will be happy with a VG+ record, especially if it is toward the high side of the grade (sometimes called VG++).

VERY GOOD (VG)

Many of the imperfections found on a VG+ record are more obvious on a VG record. That said, VG records – which usually go for no more than 25 percent of a Near Mint record – are among the biggest bargains in record collecting, because most of the "big money" goes for more perfect copies. For many listeners, a VG record will be worth the money.

The Beatles

45 RPM Singles

ACROSS THE UNIVERSE/TWO OF US

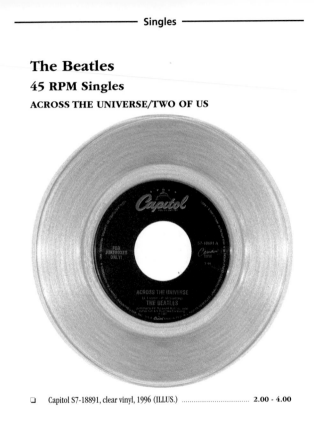

❑   Capitol S7-18891, clear vinyl, 1996 (ILLUS.) .... **2.00 - 4.00**

ACT NATURALLY/YESTERDAY

See YESTERDAY/ACT NATURALLY.

AIN'T SHE SWEET/NOBODY'S CHILD

❏ Atco 45-6308, yellow and white label, with "Vocal by John Lennon" on left of label,
1964..**25.00 - 50.00**
❏ Atco 45-6308, yellow and white label, with "Vocal by John Lennon" under "The
Beatles", 1964...**30.00 - 60.00**
❏ Atco 45-6308, white label, promotional copy, with "Vocal by John Lennon" on left
of label, 1964...**150.00 - 300.00**
❏ Atco 45-6308, white label, promotional copy, with "Vocal by John Lennon" under
"The Beatles", 1964..**150.00 - 300.00**

AIN'T SHE SWEET/SWEET GEORGIA BROWN

❏ Atlantic OS-13243, "Oldies Series", gold and black label,
1983..**5.00 - 10.00**
❏ Atlantic OS-13243, "Oldies Series", silver, red and black label,
1985..**10.00 - 20.00**

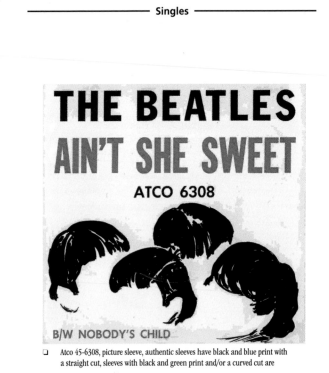

❏ Atco 45-6308, picture sleeve, authentic sleeves have black and blue print with a straight cut, sleeves with black and green print and/or a curved cut are reproductions, 1964 (ILLUS.) .... 250.00 - 500.00

ALL MY LOVING/THIS BOY

❏   Capitol 72144, orange and yellow swirl; Canadian release that was heavily
     imported to the U.S., 1964 (ILLUS.)...**25.00 - 50.00**

❏ Capitol 72144, Canadian number with U.S. labels, red and orange "target" label,

1971 ....**50.00 - 100.00**

ALL MY LOVING/YOU'VE GOT TO HIDE
YOUR LOVE AWAY

❏ Capitol/Evatone 420826cs, Flexi-disc issued as giveaway by The Musicland Group;

"Musicland" version, 1982 .... **5.00 - 10.00**

❏ Capitol/Evatone 420826cs, Flexi-disc issued as giveaway by The Musicland Group;

"Discount" version, 1982.. **10.00 - 20.00**

❏ Capitol/Evatone 420826cs, Flexi-disc issued as giveaway by The Musicland Group;

"Sam Goody" version, 1982 .... **12.50 - 25.00**

ALL YOU NEED IS LOVE/BABY, YOU'RE A RICH MAN

❏ Capitol 5964, orange and yellow swirl, without "A Subsidiary Of"... in perimeter
   label print, no comma in "Baby You're a Rich Man," two type styles exist,
   1967 (ILLUS.) .... **12.50 - 25.00**

❏ Capitol 5964, orange and yellow swirl, without "A Subsidiary Of"... in perimeter
   label print, with comma in "Baby, You're a Rich Man," 1967 .... **15.00 - 30.00**

❏ Capitol P 5964, light green label promo, 1967 .... **125.00 - 250.00**

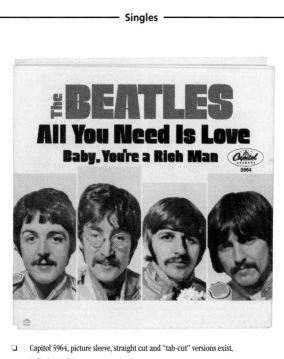

❑   Capitol 5964, picture sleeve, straight cut and "tab-cut" versions exist,
    1967 (ILLUS.) ....**20.00 - 40.00**

❏ Capitol 5964, orange and yellow swirl label with "A Subsidiary Of" in perimeter
print, 1968..**25.00 - 50.00**

❏ Capitol 5964, red and orange "target" label with Capitol dome logo,
1969..**37.50 - 75.00**

❏ Capitol 5964, red and orange "target" label with Capitol round
logo, 1969..**10.00 - 20.00**

❏ Apple 5964, with star on A-side label, "Baby, You're a Rich Man" is labeled with the
full apple, 1971..**15.00 - 30.00**

❏ Apple 5964, without star on A-side label, "Baby, You're a Rich Man" is labeled with
the full apple, 1971..**5.00 - 10.00**

❏ Apple 5964, with "All Rights Reserved" disclaimer, "Baby, You're a Rich Man" is
labeled with the full apple, 1975 ....**7.50 - 15.00**

❏ Capitol 5964, orange label with "Capitol" at bottom,
1976..**3.00 - 6.00**

❏ Capitol 5964, purple label, 1978..........................**7.50 - 15.00**

❏ Capitol Starline A-6300, blue label with "Stereo," 1981....................**4.00 - 8.00**
❏ Capitol Starline A-6300, blue label with "Mono,"
1981..**12.50 - 25.00**

❏ Capitol Starline X-6300, blue label with "Mono,"
1981..**2.50 - 5.00**

❏ Capitol Starline X-6300, black colorband label, 1986................**10.00 - 20.00**

❏ Capitol S7-17693, pink vinyl, 1994 ....**2.00 - 4.00**

AND I LOVE HER/IF I FELL

AND I LOVE HER
(John Lennon-Paul McCartney)
From the United Artists Picture, "A Hard Day's Night"

Unart Music
Corporation
& Maclen
Music, Inc.
BMI-2:29

5235
(45-X45039)
Recorded
in England
7-204

THE BEATLES

MFD. BY CAPITOL RECORDS, INC., U.S.A. • T.M. *Capitol* MARCA REG

❑ Capitol 5235, orange and yellow swirl, without "A Subsidiary Of"... in perimeter
label print; publishers listed as "Unart" and "Maclen," two type styles exist,
1964 (ILLUS.) .... **15.00 - 30.00**

❑ Capitol 5235, orange and yellow swirl, without "A Subsidiary Of"... in perimeter
label print; publishers listed as "Maclen" only, two type styles exist,
1964 .... **15.00 - 30.00**

❑ Capitol 5235, picture sleeve, straight cut and "tab-cut" versions exist, 1964 (ILLUS.) ....**60.00 - 120.00**

- ❏ Capitol 5235, Orange and yellow swirl with "A Subsidiary Of"... on perimeter print in white, 1968..**25.00 - 50.00**
- ❏ Capitol 5235, Orange and yellow swirl with "A Subsidiary Of"... on perimeter print in black, 1968..**37.50 - 75.00**
- ❏ Capitol 5235, red and orange "target" label with Capitol round logo, 1969..**30.00 - 60.00**
- ❏ Capitol 5235, red and orange "target" label with Capitol dome logo, 1969..**10.00 - 20.00**
- ❏ Apple 5235, with star on A-side label, 1971 ....**15.00 - 30.00**
- ❏ Apple 5235, without star on A-side label, 1971 ....**5.00 - 10.00**
- ❏ Apple 5235, with "All Rights Reserved" disclaimer, 1975..**7.50 - 15.00**
- ❏ Capitol 5235, orange label with "Capitol" at bottom, 1976..**3.00 - 6.00**
- ❏ Capitol 5235, purple label, 1978................................**7.50 - 15.00**
- ❏ Capitol Starline A-6283, blue label with "Stereo," 1981................**4.00 - 8.00**
- ❏ Capitol Starline A-6283, blue label with "Mono," 1981..**12.50 - 25.00**
- ❏ Capitol Starline X-6283, blue label with "Stereo," 1981................**2.50 - 5.00**
- ❏ Capitol Starline X-6283, black colorband label, 1986................**3.00 - 6.00**
- ❏ Capitol Starline X-6283, purple label, 1988................................**2.50 - 5.00**

ASK ME WHY/ANNA

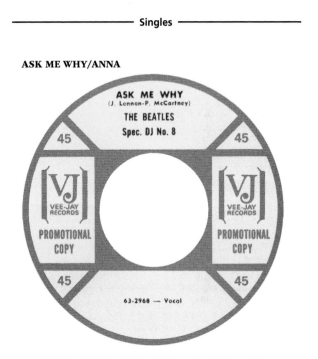

❏   Vee Jay Spec. DJ No. 8, Though it doesn't fit into any known Vee Jay numbering
    system (other "Spec. DJ No." records are rumored, but none are confirmed), this is
    an authentic 1964 promotional release, 1964 ....**7,500. – 10,000.**

ASK ME WHY/TWIST AND SHOUT

❏ Collectables 1514, recorded live in Hamburg, 1982 ....**1.00 - 3.00**

❏ Collectables 1514, picture sleeve, 1982 ....**1.00 - 3.00**

BABY, YOU'RE A RICH MAN/ALL YOU NEED IS LOVE

See ALL YOU NEED IS LOVE/BABY, YOU'RE A RICH
MAN.

THE BALLAD OF JOHN AND YOKO/OLD BROWN SHOE

❏ Apple 2531, with small Capitol logo on bottom of B-side label,
1969 ....**5.00 - 10.00**

❏ Apple 2531, with "Mfd. by Apple" on label, 1969 ....**5.00 - 10.00**

❑   Apple 2531, picture sleeve, 1969 (ILLUS.) ....**50.00 - 100.00**

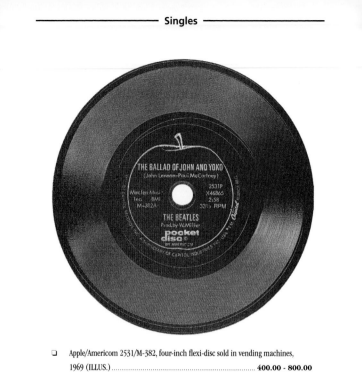

❏ Apple/Americom 2531/M-382, four-inch flexi-disc sold in vending machines, 1969 (ILLUS.) .... **400.00 - 800.00**

❏ Apple 2531, with "All Rights Reserved" disclaimer,
1975 ....**10.00 - 20.00**
❏ Capitol 2531, orange label with "Capitol" at bottom; should exist, but not known to
exist, 1976 .... **— - —**
❏ Capitol 2531, purple label; notches along label's edge,
1978 ....**3.00 - 6.00**
❏ Capitol 2531, Black label with colorband, 1983 ....**3.50 - 7.00**
❏ Capitol 2531, purple label; label has smooth edge,
1988 ....**3.00 - 6.00**

BE-BOP-A-LULA/HALLELUJAH I LOVE HER SO

❏ Collectables 1510, recorded live in Hamburg, 1982 ....**1.00 - 3.00**
❏ Collectables 1510, picture sleeve, 1982 ....**1.00 - 3.00**

THE BEATLES 1968 CHRISTMAS RECORD

❑   Beatles Fan Club (1968) H-2041, flexi-disc made by Americom,
       1968 (ILLUS.) .... **30.00 - 60.00**

☐ Beatles Fan Club (1968) H-2041, picture sleeve,
1968 (ILLUS.) ....**37.50 - 70.00**

THE BEATLES' MOVIE MEDLEY/FAB FOUR ON FILM

- ❏ Capitol B-5100, stock copy; not officially released, but some "escaped," 1982 .... **25.00 - 50.00**
- ❏ Capitol PB-5100, promotional copy, 1982 .... **12.50 - 25.00**
- ❏ Capitol B-5100, picture sleeve, 1982 .... **10.00 - 20.00**

THE BEATLES' MOVIE MEDLEY/I'M HAPPY JUST TO DANCE WITH YOU

- ❏ Capitol B-5107, 1982 .... **2.50 - 5.00**
- ❏ Capitol B-5107, picture sleeve, 1982 .... **2.50 - 5.00**

BIRTHDAY/TAXMAN

- ❏ Capitol S7-17488, black vinyl "error" pressing, 1994 ..... **25.00 - 50.00**
- ❏ Capitol S7-17488, green vinyl, 1994 .... **2.00 - 4.00**

BOYS/KANSAS CITY

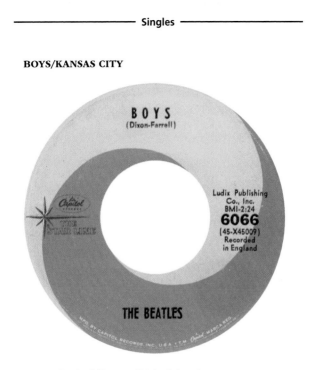

❏ Capitol Starline 6066, green swirl label, 1965 (ILLUS.) .... **40.00 - 80.00**

❏ Capitol 6066, red and orange "target" label, 1971 .... **15.00 - 30.00**

CAN'T BUY ME LOVE/YOU CAN'T DO THAT

❑ Capitol 5150, orange and yellow swirl, without "A Subsidiary Of"... in perimeter
label print, two type styles exist, 1964 .... **15.00 - 30.00**

❑ Capitol 5150, yellow and black vinyl (unauthorized),
1964 (ILLUS.) .... **1,500. – 2,000.**

❑ Capitol 5150, yellow vinyl (unauthorized), 1964 .... **3,000. – 4,000.**

❏   Capitol 5150, picture sleeve, numerous counterfeits exist; all legitimate copies have
     a straight cut, titles in black and George Harrison's entire head pictured, while
     counterfeits have a blurry cover picture, some have Harrison's head cut off, and
     some have the titles in red; other counterfeits are difficult to distinguish from the
     real thing; if in doubt, buy from or consult an expert,

     1964 (ILLUS.) .... **400.00 - 800.00**

❏ Capitol 5150, orange and yellow swirl label with "A Subsidiary Of" in perimeter print, two type styles exist, 1968 .... **25.00 - 50.00**

❏ Capitol 5150, red and orange "target" label, round logo, 1969 .... **30.00 - 60.00**

❏ Capitol 5150, red and orange "target" label, dome logo, 1969 .... **12.50 - 25.00**

❏ Apple 5150, with star on A-side label, 1971 .... **15.00 - 30.00**

❏ Apple 5150, without star on A-side label, 1971 .... **5.00 - 10.00**

❏ Apple 5150, with "All Rights Reserved" disclaimer on label, 1975 .... **7.50 - 15.00**

❏ Capitol 5150, orange label with "Capitol" at bottom, 1976 .... **3.00 - 6.00**

❏ Capitol 5150, purple label, 1978 .... **7.50 - 15.00**

❏ Capitol Starline A-6279, blue label with "Stereo," 1981 .... **4.00 - 8.00**

❏ Capitol Starline A-6279, blue label with "Mono," 1981 .... **12.50 - 25.00**

❏ Capitol Starline X-6279, blue label with "Mono," 1981 .... **2.50 - 5.00**

❏ Capitol Starline X-6279, black label with colorband, 1986 .... **3.00 - 6.00**

❏ Capitol Starline X-6279, purple label, 1988 .... **2.50 - 5.00**

❏ Capitol S7-17690, green vinyl, 1994 .... **2.00 - 4.00**

CHRISTMAS TIME IS HERE AGAIN!

❏ Beatles Fan Club (1967), postcard, title is on the typed side, the side that is played
simply says "Season's Greetings from the Beatles" without a year,
1967 (ILLUS.) ....**75.00 - 150.00**

CRY FOR A SHADOW/ROCK AND ROLL MUSIC

❏ Collectables 1520, Despite label credit to The Beatles, B-side is a Peter Best

recording, 1987 ....**2.50 - 5.00**

CRYING, WAITING, HOPING/TAKE GOOD CARE OF MY BABY

❏ Backstage 1155, promo-only picture disc in plastic sleeve; these songs are from the

1962 Decca audition tape, 1983 ....**12.50 - 25.00**

DECADE

❏ (no label) MBRF-55551, a bootleg of radio spots for the Beatles' back catalog,

compiled without authorization by two former Capitol employees., 1974 .... **— - —**

DIALOGUE FROM THE BEATLES' MOTION PICTURE "LET IT BE"

DIALOGUE FROM THE
BEATLES' MOTION PICTURE
"LET IT BE"

BEATLES
PROMO-
1970

Manufactured by Apple Records Inc.,
1700 Broadway, New York, N.Y. 10019
An **abkco** managed company

❑   Apple Promo-1970 [DJ], 1970 (ILLUS.) ....**30.00 - 60.00**

DO YOU WANT TO KNOW A SECRET/THANK YOU GIRL

- ❏ Vee Jay 587, black rainbow label, oval logo, 1964 (ILLUS.)............. **25.00 - 50.00**
- ❏ Vee Jay 587, black rainbow label, brackets logo, four type styles exist, 1964 .... **20.00 - 40.00**

❏ Vee Jay 587, plain black label with two horizontal lines; "VJ" in brackets, 1964 .... **22.50 - 45.00**

❏ Vee Jay 587, plain black label; "Vee Jay" in oval, 1964 .... **32.50 - 65.00**

❏ Vee Jay 587, plain black label; "VEE JAY" stands alone, 1964 .... **25.00 - 50.00**

❏ Vee Jay 587, plain black label; "VJ" by itself with "VEE JAY RECORDS" under it in small type, 1964 .... **32.50 - 65.00**

❏ Vee Jay 587, plain black label; "VJ" in brackets, authentic copies have "Do You Want to Know a Secret" on two lines, versions that may be counterfeit have "Do You Want to Know a Secret" on one line, 1964 .... **32.50 - 65.00**

❏ Vee Jay 587, yellow label, 1964 .... **32.50 - 65.00**

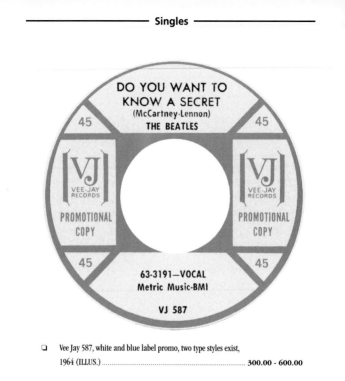

❏   Vee Jay 587, white and blue label promo, two type styles exist,
     1964 (ILLUS.) .... **300.00 - 600.00**

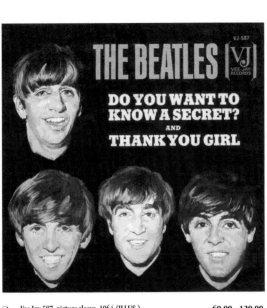

❏ Vee Jay 587, picture sleeve, 1964 (ILLUS.) ....**60.00 - 120.00**
❏ Oldies 45 149, authentic copies have "Oldies 45" in white, counterfeits have "Oldies 45" in black, 1964 .... **7.50 - 15.00**
❏ Capitol Starline 6064, green swirl label, two type styles exist, 1965 ....**60.00 - 120.00**

EIGHT DAYS A WEEK/I DON'T WANT TO SPOIL THE PARTY

❏   Capitol 5371, orange and yellow swirl, without "A Subsidiary Of"... in perimeter
label print, two type styles exist, 1965 ....**15.00 - 30.00**

❏   Capitol 5371, orange and yellow swirl, without "A Subsidiary Of"... in perimeter
label print, with 360 notches along edge of label, 1968 ....**20.00 - 40.00**

❏   Capitol 5371, picture sleeve, straight-cut sleeve, 1965 (ILLUS.) ......**37.50 - 75.00**

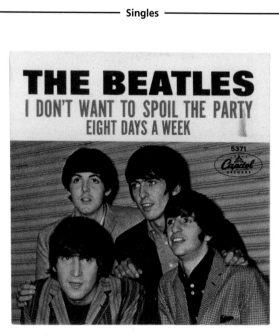

❑ Capitol 5371, picture sleeve, die-cut sleeve, 1965 (ILLUS.) .... **12.50 - 25.00**

❏ Capitol 5371, orange and yellow swirl label with "A Subsidiary Of" in perimeter print, 1968..**25.00 - 50.00**

❏ Capitol 5371, red and orange "target" label with Capitol dome logo, 1969..**30.00 - 60.00**

❏ Capitol 5371, red and orange "target" label with Capitol round logo, 1969..**10.00 - 20.00**

❏ Apple 5371, with star on A-side label, 1971 ....**15.00 - 30.00**

❏ Apple 5371, without star on A-side label, 1971 ....**5.00 - 10.00**

❏ Apple 5371, with "All Rights Reserved" disclaimer, 1975..**7.50 - 15.00**

❏ Capitol 5371, orange label with "Capitol" at bottom, 1976.................**3.00 - 6.00**

❏ Capitol 5371, purple label, 1978..**7.50 - 15.00**

❏ Capitol Starline A-6287, blue label with "Stereo," 1981....................**4.00 - 8.00**

❏ Capitol Starline A-6287, blue label with "Mono," 1981 ....**12.50 - 25.00**

❏ Capitol Starline X-6287, blue label with "Mono," 1981....................**2.50 - 5.00**

❏ Capitol Starline X-6287, black colorband label, 1986........................**2.50 - 5.00**

❏ Capitol Starline X-6287, purple label, 1988......................................**2.50 - 5.00**

EVERYWHERE IT'S CHRISTMAS

See 1966: SEASON'S GREETINGS FROM THE BEATLES.

FALLING IN LOVE AGAIN/SHEILA

❏ Collectables 1509, recorded live in Hamburg,1982............................**1.00 - 3.00**

❏ Collectables 1509, picture sleeve, 1982 ....**1.00 - 3.00**

FREE AS A BIRD/CHRISTMAS TIME (IS HERE AGAIN)

❏   Apple 58497, small center hole, 1995...**2.00 - 4.00**

❏   Apple 58497, picture sleeve, 1995 (ILLUS.) ....**2.00 - 4.00**

FROM ME TO YOU/THANK YOU GIRL

(NOTE: This record was not issued with a picture sleeve; bootleg picture
sleeves exist.)

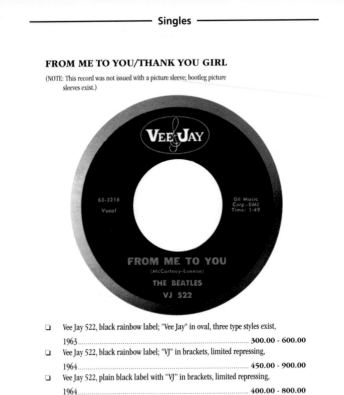

- ☐ Vee Jay 522, black rainbow label; "Vee Jay" in oval, three type styles exist,
  1963 .... **300.00 - 600.00**
- ☐ Vee Jay 522, black rainbow label; "VJ" in brackets, limited repressing,
  1964 .... **450.00 - 900.00**
- ☐ Vee Jay 522, plain black label with "VJ" in brackets, limited repressing,
  1964 .... **400.00 - 800.00**
- ☐ Vee Jay 522, "Disc Jockey Advance Sample," white label,
  1963 .... **250.00 - 500.00**

GERMAN MEDLEY

❏ Capitol/Evatone 1214825cs, Flexi-disc given away by House of Guitars in New York, 1983 .... **30.00 - 60.00**

GET BACK/DON'T LET ME DOWN

❏ Apple 2490, no times listed on labels, with small Capitol logo on bottom of B-side label, 1969 (ILLUS.) .... **10.00 - 20.00**

❏ Apple/Americom 2490/M-335, four-inch flexi-disc sold in vending
machines, 1969 (ILLUS.) ....**500.00 – 1,000.**

❑ Apple 2490, with small Capitol logo on bottom of B-side label,

1969 .... **5.00 - 10.00**

❑ Apple 2490, with "Mfd. by Apple" on label, 1969 .... **5.00 - 10.00**

❑ Apple 2490, with "All Rights Reserved" disclaimer,

1975 .... **10.00 - 20.00**

❑ Capitol 2490, orange label with "Capitol" at bottom,

1976 .... **3.00 - 6.00**

❑ Capitol 2490, purple label; notches along label's edge,

1978 .... **4.00 - 8.00**

❑ Capitol 2490, black label with colorband; "Get Back" replaced by LP version as on

Let It Be, 1983 .... **3.00 - 6.00**

❑ Capitol 2490, purple label; label has smooth edge; "Get Back" replaced by LP

version as on Let It Be, 1988 .... **2.50 - 5.00**

GIRL (MONO/STEREO)

❑ Capitol P-4506, promo only; black vinyl; all colored vinyl versions are counterfeits,

1977 .... **100.00 - 200.00**

GIRL/YOU'RE GOING TO LOSE THAT GIRL

❑ Capitol 4506, picture sleeve; 16,000 were made; though labels were printed, no
   records ever were, so all records with both songs on it are bootlegs,
   1977 (ILLUS.) .... **7.50 - 15.00**

GOT TO GET YOU INTO MY LIFE (MONO/STEREO)

❑ Capitol P-4274, promo version, 1976..**20.00 - 40.00**

GOT TO GET YOU INTO MY LIFE/HELTER SKELTER

Also see HELTER SKELTER (MONO/STEREO).

❑ Capitol 4274, orange label with "Capitol" at bottom, George Martin's name not on label, 1976...**3.00 - 6.00**

❑ Capitol 4274, orange label with "Capitol" at bottom, George Martin's name is on label, 1976..**5.00 - 10.00**

- ☐ Capitol 4274, picture sleeve, 1976 (ILLUS.)..............................**2.50 - 5.00**
- ☐ Capitol 4274, purple label; 360 notches along label's edge, 1978........**3.00 - 6.00**
- ☐ Capitol 4274, black label with colorband, 1983..............................**3.00 - 6.00**
- ☐ Capitol 4274, purple label; label has smooth edge,
  1988..**2.50 - 5.00**
- ☐ Capitol S7-18899, gold/orange vinyl, 1996 ....**2.00 - 4.00**

HAPPY CHRISTMAS 1969

❏ Beatles Fan Club (1969) H-2565, flexi-disc made by Americom,
1969 (ILLUS.) .... **20.00 - 40.00**

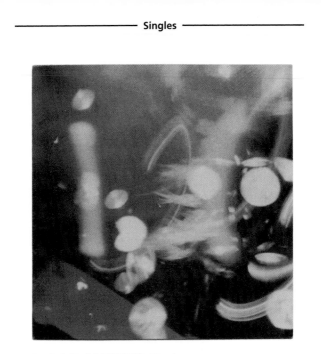

❏ Beatles Fan Club (1969) H-2565, picture sleeve,
1969 (ILLUS.) .... **30.00 - 60.00**

A HARD DAY'S NIGHT OPEN END INTERVIEW

❏ United Artists UAEP 10029, white label promo only, small hole,
  1964 (ILLUS.) .... **1,000. – 1.500.**
❏ Cicadelic/BIOdisc 001, limited edition of 700; lower numbers increase value
  substantially, 1990 .... **7.50 - 15.00**
❏ Cicadelic/BIOdisc 001, "Records Etc." pressing, 1990 .... **15.00 - 30.00**

A HARD DAY'S NIGHT THEATRE LOBBY SPOT

❏ United Artists SP-2357, promo only, 1964 (ILLUS.) .... **1,000. – 1.500.**

A HARD DAY'S NIGHT/I SHOULD HAVE KNOWN BETTER

❑ Capitol 5222, orange and yellow swirl, without "A Subsidiary Of"... in perimeter label print; first version credited both "Unart" and "Maclen" as publishers, two type styles exist, 1964 (ILLUS.) .... **15.00 - 30.00**

❑ Capitol 5222, orange and yellow swirl, without "A Subsidiary Of"... in perimeter label print; second version credited only "Maclen" as publishers, two type styles exist,1964 .... **15.00 - 30.00**

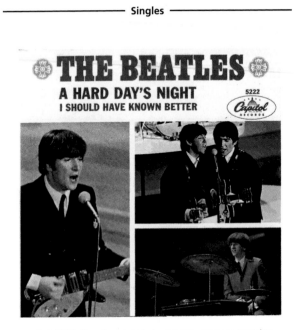

❏ Capitol 5222, picture sleeve, straight cut or "tab cut" versions exist, counterfeits also exist, 1964 (ILLUS.) .... **50.00 - 100.00**

❑ Capitol 5222, orange and yellow swirl with "A Subsidiary Of"... on perimeter print in white, two type styles exist, 1968..**25.00 - 50.00**

❑ Capitol 5222, orange and yellow swirl with "A Subsidiary Of"... on perimeter print in black, 1968..**50.00 - 100.00**

❑ Capitol 5222, red and orange "target" label with Capitol dome logo, 1969..**30.00 - 60.00**

❑ Capitol 5222, red and orange "target" label with Capitol round logo, 1969..**10.00 - 20.00**

❑ Apple 5222, with star on A-side label, 1971 ....**15.00 - 30.00**

❑ Apple 5222, without star on A-side label, 1971 ....**5.00 - 10.00**

❑ Apple 5222, with "All Rights Reserved" disclaimer, 1975..**7.50 - 15.00**

❑ Capitol 5222, orange label with "Capitol" at bottom, 1976..**3.00 - 6.00**

❑ Capitol 5222, purple label, 1978..**7.50 - 15.00**

❑ Capitol Starline A-6281, blue label with "Stereo," 1981..**4.00 - 8.00**

❑ Capitol Starline A-6281, blue label with "Mono," 1981..**12.50 - 25.00**

❑ Capitol Starline X-6281, blue label with "Mono," 1981 ....**2.50 - 5.00**

❑ Capitol Starline X-6281, black colorband label, 1986..**3.00 - 6.00**

❑ Capitol Starline X-6281, purple label, 1988..**2.50 - 5.00**

A HARD DAY'S NIGHT/THINGS WE SAID TODAY

❑ Capitol S7-17692, white vinyl, 1994..**2.00 - 4.00**

HELLO GOODBYE/I AM THE WALRUS

❑ Capitol 2056, orange and yellow swirl, without "A Subsidiary Of"... in perimeter label print; publishing credited to "Maclen" on both sides, three type styles exist, 1967..**15.00 - 30.00**

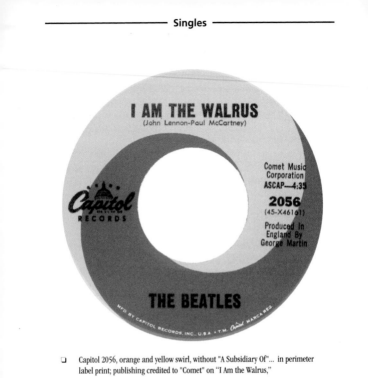

❑ Capitol 2056, orange and yellow swirl, without "A Subsidiary Of"... in perimeter
label print; publishing credited to "Comet" on "I Am the Walrus,"
1967 (ILLUS.) .... **15.00 - 30.00**

- ❏ Capitol 2056, orange and yellow swirl, without "A Subsidiary Of"... in perimeter label print; publishing credited to "Comet" on "Hello Goodbye," two type styles exist, 1967 (ILLUS.) .... **15.00 - 30.00**
- ❏ Capitol 2056, orange and yellow swirl, without "A Subsidiary Of"... in perimeter label print; publishing credited to "Comet" on both sides, each label has a different type style, 1967 .... **20.00 - 40.00**
- ❏ Capitol P 2056, light green label promo, 1967 .... **125.00 - 250.00**

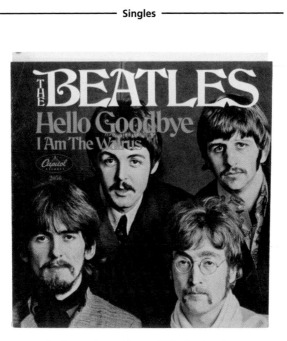

❏ Capitol 2056, picture sleeve, straight cut and "tab-cut" versions exist,
1967 (ILLUS.) ....**50.00 - 100.00**

❏ Capitol 2056, orange and yellow swirl label with "A Subsidiary Of" in perimeter print, 1968...**25.00 - 50.00**

❏ Capitol 2056, red and orange "target" label with Capitol dome logo, 1969..**30.00 - 60.00**

❏ Capitol 2056, red and orange "target" label with Capitol round logo, 1969..**10.00 - 20.00**

❏ Apple 2056, with star on A-side label, 1971 ....**15.00 - 30.00**

❏ Apple 2056, without star on A-side label, 1971 ....**5.00 - 10.00**

❏ Apple 2056, with "All Rights Reserved" disclaimer, 1975..**10.00 - 20.00**

❏ Capitol 2056, orange label with "Capitol" at bottom, 1976..**3.00 - 6.00**

❏ Capitol 2056, purple label; notches along label's edge, 1978..**4.00 - 8.00**

❏ Capitol 2056, black colorband label, 1983 ....**3.00 - 6.00**

❏ Capitol 2056, purple label; smooth label edge, 1988 ....**2.50 - 5.00**

HELP! OPEN END INTERVIEW

❏ Cicadelic/BIOdisc 002, 1990 ....**2.50 - 5.00**

❏ Cicadelic/BIOdisc 002, picture sleeve, 1990...................................**2.50 - 5.00**

HELP!/I'M DOWN

❑ Capitol 5476, orange and yellow swirl, without "A Subsidiary Of"... in perimeter
label print, only "Maclen" is listed as publisher of "Help!," two type styles exist,
1965 (ILLUS.) .... **15.00 - 30.00**

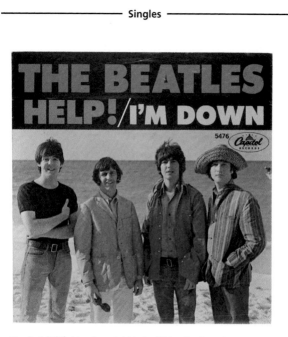

❏ Capitol 5476, picture sleeve, straight cut and "tab-cut" versions exist,
1965 (ILLUS.) ....**37.50 - 75.00**

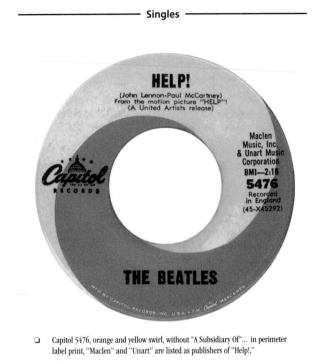

❏ Capitol 5476, orange and yellow swirl, without "A Subsidiary Of"... in perimeter label print, "Maclen" and "Unart" are listed as publishers of "Help!," 1967?..**25.00 - 50.00**

❑ Capitol 5476, orange and yellow swirl with "A Subsidiary Of"... on perimeter print in white, 1968..**25.00 - 50.00**

❑ Capitol 5476, orange and yellow swirl with "A Subsidiary Of"... on perimeter print in black, 1968...**50.00 - 100.00**

❑ Capitol 5476, red and orange "target" label with Capitol dome logo, 1969...**30.00 - 60.00**

❑ Capitol 5476, red and orange "target" label with Capitol round logo, 1969...**10.00 - 20.00**

❑ Apple 5476, with star on A-side label, 1971 ....**15.00 - 30.00**

❑ Apple 5476, without star on A-side label, 1971 ....**5.00 - 10.00**

❑ Apple 5476, with "All Rights Reserved" disclaimer, 1975..**7.50 - 15.00**

❑ Capitol 5476, orange label with "Capitol" at bottom, 1976..**3.00 - 6.00**

❑ Capitol 5476, purple label, 1978.......................................**7.50 - 15.00**

❑ Capitol Starline A-6290, blue label with "Stereo," 1981......................**4.00 - 8.00**

❑ Capitol Starline A-6290, blue label with "Mono," 1981..**12.50 - 25.00**

❑ Capitol Starline X-6290, blue label with "Mono," 1981 ....**3.00 - 6.00**

❑ Capitol Starline X-6290, black colorband label, 1986........................**3.00 - 6.00**

❑ Capitol Starline X-6290, purple label, 1988......................**2.50 - 5.00**

❑ Capitol S7-17691, white vinyl, 1994..................................**2.00 - 4.00**

HELTER SKELTER (MONO/STEREO)

Also see GOT TO GET YOU INTO MY LIFE/HELTER SKELTER.

❑ Capitol P-4274, promo only, 1976 ....**20.00 - 40.00**

HERE COMES THE SUN/OCTOPUS'S GARDEN

❏   Capitol S7-17700, gold/orange vinyl, 1994 ....**2.00 - 4.00**

HERE, THERE AND EVERYWHERE/GOOD DAY SUNSHINE

❏   Capitol S7-18897, yellow vinyl, 1996 (ILLUS.) ....**2.00 - 4.00**

HEY JUDE/REVOLUTION

❏ Apple 2276, first editions have no matrix numbers under "2276" on either side and do not mention George Martin or "Recorded in England,"

1968 (ILLUS.) .... **25.00 - 50.00**

REVOLUTION

(Lennon & McCartney)

Produced by: George Martin

2276

THE BEATLES

Maclen Music Inc., BMI

3:22

❑   Apple 2276, with no matrix numbers under "2276" but WITH "Produced by George
Martin" and "Recorded in England" credit, with small Capitol logo on B-side label,
1968 (ILLUS.) .... **12.50 - 25.00**

❏ Apple 2276, with no matrix numbers under "2276" but WITH "Produced by George Martin" and "Recorded in England" credit, "Mfd. by Apple" on B-side label, 1968 .... **10.00 - 20.00**

❏ Apple 2276, with matrix numbers under "2276" but WITHOUT "Produced by George Martin" and "Recorded in England" credit, 1968 .... **10.00 - 20.00**

❏ Apple 2276, with all credits, with small Capitol logo on bottom of B-side label, 1968 .... **7.50 - 15.00**

❏ Apple 2276, with all credits, with "Mfd. by Apple" on label, 1968 .... **5.00 - 10.00**

❏ Apple/Americom 2276/M-221, Four-inch flexi-disc sold in vending machines; "Hey Jude" is edited to 3:25, 1969 .... **150.00 - 300.00**

❏ Apple 2276, with "All Rights Reserved" disclaimer,
   1975 ....**10.00 - 20.00**
❏ Capitol 2276, orange label with "Capitol" at bottom,
   1976 ....**3.00 - 6.00**
❏ Capitol 2276, purple label; notches along label's edge,
   1978 ....**4.00 - 8.00**
❏ Capitol 2276, black label with colorband, 1983 ....**3.00 - 6.00**
❏ Capitol 2276, purple label; label has smooth edge,
   1988 ....**2.50 - 5.00**
❏ Capitol S7-17694, blue vinyl, 1994 ....**2.00 - 4.00**

HIPPY HIPPY SHAKE/SWEET LITTLE SIXTEEN

❏ Collectables 1502, recorded live in Hamburg,1982 ....**1.00 - 3.00**
❏ Collectables 1502, picture sleeve, 1982 ....**1.00 - 3.00**

HOW'D YOU GET TO KNOW HER NAME/IF YOU CAN'T GET HER

❏ Collectables 1519, Despite label credit to The Beatles, both are Peter Best
   recordings, 1987 ....**5.00 - 10.00**

I FEEL FINE/SHE'S A WOMAN

❏ Capitol 5327, orange and yellow swirl, without "A Subsidiary Of"... in perimeter
   label print, two type styles exist, 1964 ....**15.00 - 30.00**

❏   Capitol 5327, picture sleeve, straight cut or "tab cut" versions exist,
1964 (ILLUS.) .... **40.00 - 80.00**

❏ Capitol 5327, orange and yellow swirl label with "A Subsidiary Of" in perimeter
print, two type styles exist, 1968 ....**25.00 - 50.00**

❏ Capitol 5327, red and orange "target" label with Capitol round logo,
1969 ....**30.00 - 60.00**

❏ Capitol 5327, red and orange "target" label with Capitol dome logo,
1969 ....**10.00 - 20.00**

❏ Apple 5327, with star on A-side label, 1971 ....**15.00 - 30.00**

❏ Apple 5327, without star on A-side label, 1971 ....**5.00 - 10.00**

❏ Apple 5327, with "All Rights Reserved" disclaimer,
1975 ....**7.50 - 15.00**

❏ Capitol 5327, orange label with "Capitol" at bottom,
1976 ....**3.00 - 6.00**

❏ Capitol 5327, purple label, 1978 ....**7.50 - 15.00**

❏ Capitol Starline A-6286, blue label with "Stereo," 1981 ....**4.00 - 8.00**

❏ Capitol Starline A-6286, blue label with "Mono,"
1981 ....**12.50 - 25.00**

❏ Capitol Starline X-6286, blue label with "Mono," 1981 ....**2.50 - 5.00**

❏ Capitol Starline X-6286, black colorband label, 1986 ....**3.00 - 6.00**

❏ Capitol Starline X-6286, purple label, 1988 ....**2.50 - 5.00**

I SAW HER STANDING THERE/CAN'T HELP IT "BLUE ANGEL"

❏ Collectables 1515, B-side is actually "Reminiscing"; recorded live in Hamburg,
1982 ....**1.00 - 3.00**

❏ Collectables 1515, picture sleeve, 1982 ....**1.00 - 3.00**

I WANT TO HOLD YOUR HAND (MONO/STEREO)

❏ Capitol 7PRO-9076/ P-5112, promo, 1984 ....**7.50 - 15.00**

I WANT TO HOLD YOUR HAND/I SAW HER STANDING THERE

- ❏ Capitol 5112, first pressing credits "Walter Hofer" as B-side publisher, two type
  styles exist, 1964 (ILLUS.) .... **20.00 - 40.00**
- ❏ Capitol 5112, second pressing credits "George Pincus & Sons Music Corp. ASCAP"
  as B-side publisher, two type styles exist, 1964 .... **17.50 - 35.00**
- ❏ Capitol 5112, third pressing credits "Gil Music Corp. BMI" as B-side publisher, two
  type styles exist, 1964 .... **15.00 - 30.00**

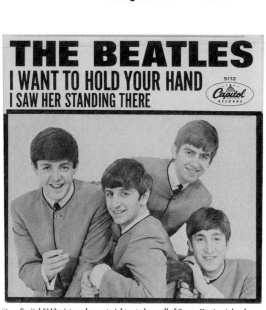

❑ Capitol 5112, picture sleeve, straight cut, shows all of George Harrison's head, 1964 (ILLUS.) ....**50.00 - 100.00**

❏ Capitol 5112, picture sleeve, die-cut, crops George Harrison's head in photo, 1964 .... **50.00 - 100.00**

❏ Capitol 5112, orange and yellow swirl label with "A Subsidiary Of Capitol Industries" in perimeter print, 1968 .... **30.00 - 60.00**

❏ Capitol 5112, red and orange "target" label, dome logo, 1969 .... **30.00 - 60.00**

❏ Capitol 5112, red and orange "target" label, round logo, 1969 .... **12.50 - 25.00**

❏ Apple 5112, with star on label, 1971 .... **15.00 - 30.00**

❏ Apple 5112, without star on label, 1971 .... **5.00 - 10.00**

❏ Apple 5112, with "All Rights Reserved" disclaimer on label, 1975 .... **10.00 - 20.00**

❏ Capitol 5112, orange label, "Capitol" logo on bottom, 1976 .... **5.00 - 10.00**

❏ Capitol 5112, purple label, 1978 .... **7.50 - 15.00**

❏ Capitol Starline A-6278, blue labels that say "Stereo," 1981 .... **10.00 - 20.00**

❏ Capitol Starline A-6278, blue labels that say "Mono," 1981 .... **12.50 - 25.00**

❏ Capitol Starline X-6278, blue labels that say "Mono," 1982 .... **6.00 - 12.00**

❏ Capitol 5112, 20th anniversary reissue; black print on perimeter of label, 1984 .... **2.50 - 5.00**

❏ Capitol 5112, picture sleeve, same as 1964 sleeve except has "1984" in small print, and Paul McCartney's cigarette is airbrushed out, 1984 .... **3.00 - 6.00**

❏ Capitol 5112, 30th anniversary reissue; has "7243-8-58123-7-8" engraved in record's trail-off area, 1994 .... **2.50 - 5.00**

❏ Capitol 5112, picture sleeve, same as 1964 sleeve except "Reg. U.S. Pat. Off." has periods (1964s do not); also came with a plastic sleeve with a "30th Anniversary" and UPC stickers (add 25%), 1994 .... **2.00 - 4.00**

I WANT TO HOLD YOUR HAND/THIS BOY

❏   Capitol S7-17689, clear vinyl, 1994 ....**2.00 - 4.00**

I WANT TO HOLD YOUR HAND/WMCA GOOD GUYS

❏   Capitol 5112, picture sleeve, giveaway from New York radio station with regular
Beatles photo on front and photo of "WMCA Good Guys" DJs on rear,
1964 (ILLUS.) ....**1,500. – 2,000.**

I'LL CRY INSTEAD/I'M HAPPY JUST TO DANCE WITH YOU

❏   Capitol 5234, orange and yellow swirl, without "A Subsidiary Of"... in perimeter
label print, two type styles exist,1964 (ILLUS.) .... **20.00 - 40.00**

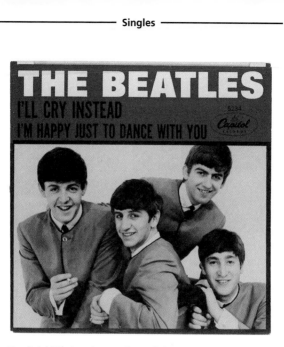

❑ Capitol 5234, picture sleeve, straight cut or "tab cut" versions exist, 1964 (ILLUS.) ....**75.00 - 150.00**

❏ Capitol 5234, orange and yellow swirl label with "A Subsidiary Of" in perimeter print, 1968...**30.00 - 60.00**

❏ Capitol 5234, red and orange "target" label with Capitol dome logo, 1969..**37.50 - 70.00**

❏ Capitol 5234, red and orange "target" label with Capitol round logo, 1969..**10.00 - 20.00**

❏ Apple 5234, with star on A-side label, 1971 ....**15.00 - 30.00**

❏ Apple 5234, without star on A-side label, 1971 ....**5.00 - 10.00**

❏ Apple 5234, with "All Rights Reserved" disclaimer, 1975..**7.50 - 15.00**

❏ Capitol 5234, orange label with "Capitol" at bottom, 1976..**3.00 - 6.00**

❏ Capitol 5234, purple label, 1978..**7.50 - 15.00**

❏ Capitol Starline A-6282, blue label with "Stereo," 1981.....................**4.00 - 8.00**

❏ Capitol Starline A-6282, blue label with "Mono," 1981..**12.50 - 25.00**

❏ Capitol Starline X-6282, blue label with "Mono," 1981 ....**3.00 - 6.00**

❏ Capitol Starline X-6282, black colorband label, 1986........................**3.00 - 6.00**

❏ Capitol Starline X-6282, purple label, 1988.....................................**3.00 - 6.00**

I'LL GET YOU (ONE-SIDED)

Also see SHE LOVES YOU/I'LL GET YOU.

❏ Swan 4152, promo only, white label with black print, four slight variations exist, each of roughly equal value, 1964..**400.00 - 600.00**

I'LL HAVE EVERYTHING TOO/I'M CHECKING OUT NOW BABY

❑ Collectables 1518, despite label credit to The Beatles, both are Peter Best recordings, 1987 .... **5.00 - 10.00**

I'LL TRY ANYWAY/I DON'T KNOW WHY I DO (I JUST DO)

❑ Collectables 1516, despite label credit to The Beatles, both are Peter Best recordings, 1987 .... **5.00 - 10.00**

I'M GONNA SIT RIGHT DOWN AND CRY OVER YOU/ ROLL OVER BEETHOVEN

❑ Collectables 1501, recorded live in Hamburg, 1982 .... **1.00 - 3.00**

❑ Collectables 1501, picture sleeve, 1982 .... **1.00 - 3.00**

IT'S ALL TOO MUCH/ONLY A NORTHERN SONG

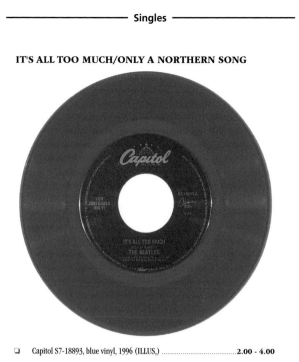

❏   Capitol S7-18893, blue vinyl, 1996 (ILLUS,) ....**2.00 - 4.00**

KANSAS CITY-HEY HEY HEY HEY/AIN'T NOTHING SHAKIN LIKE THE LEAVES ON A TREE

❏   Collectables 1507, recorded live in Hamburg, 1982............................**1.00 - 3.00**
❏   Collectables 1507, picture sleeve, 1982 ....**1.00 - 3.00**

LADY MADONNA/THE INNER LIGHT

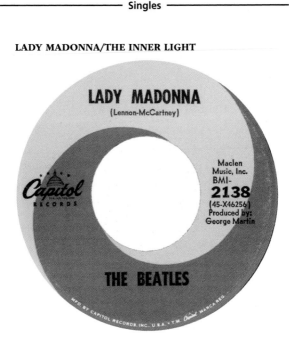

❏ Capitol 2138, orange and yellow swirl, without "A Subsidiary Of"... in perimeter
   label print, no times listed on labels, 1968 (ILLUS.) .... **25.00 - 50.00**
❏ Capitol 2138, orange and yellow swirl, without "A Subsidiary Of"... in perimeter
   label print, times listed on labels, three type styles exist, 1968 .... **15.00 - 30.00**
❏ Capitol P 2138, light green label promo, 1968 .... **100.00 - 200.00**

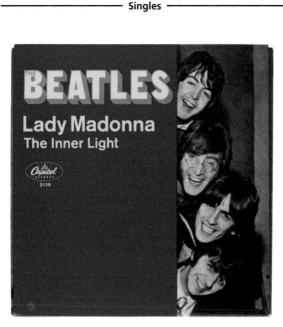

❏   Capitol 2138, picture sleeve, 1968 (ILLUS.) ....**50.00 - 100.00**

❑ Capitol 2138, picture sleeve, "Beatles Fan Club" insert that was issued with above sleeve, originals are glossy., 1968 (ILLUS.) .... **10.00 - 20.00**

- Capitol 2138, orange and yellow swirl label with "A Subsidiary Of" in perimeter print, 1968..**25.00 - 50.00**
- Capitol 2138, red and orange "target" label with Capitol dome logo, 1969..**30.00 - 60.00**
- Capitol 2138, red and orange "target" label with Capitol round logo, 1969..**10.00 - 20.00**
- Apple 2138, without star on A-side label, 1971 ....**5.00 - 10.00**
- Apple 2138, with star on A-side label, 1971 ....**15.00 - 30.00**
- Apple 2138, with "All Rights Reserved" disclaimer, 1975..**10.00 - 20.00**
- Capitol 2138, orange label with "Capitol" at bottom, 1976..**3.00 - 6.00**
- Capitol 2138, purple label; notches along label's edge, 1978..**4.00 - 8.00**
- Capitol 2138, black label with colorband, 1983................................**3.00 - 6.00**
- Capitol 2138, purple label; label has smooth edge, 1988..**2.50 - 5.00**

LEAVE MY KITTEN ALONE/OB-LA-DI, OB-LA-DA

THE BEATLES   LEAVE MY KITTEN ALONE

❑   Capitol B-5439, picture sleeve for a record that was never released, not even as a
    promo, 1985 (ILLUS.) ....**25.00 - 50.00**

LEND ME YOUR COMB/YOUR FEETS TOO BIG

❑   Collectables 1503, recorded live in Hamburg, 1982 ....**1.00 - 3.00**
❑   Collectables 1503, picture sleeve, 1982 ....**1.00 - 3.00**

LET IT BE RADIO SPOTS

United Artists

Entertainment from
Transamerica Corporation

LET IT BE

33 1/3 RPM   ULP42370

Cut 1------:60 seconds
Cut 2------:30 seconds
Cut 3------:10 seconds

❑   United Artists ULP-42370, 1970 (ILLUS.) ....**800.00 – 1,200.**

LET IT BE/YOU KNOW MY NAME (LOOK UP MY NUMBER)

❑   Apple 2764, with small Capitol logo on bottom of B-side label, three layout
     variations exist, 1970 ....**6.00 - 12.00**
❑   Apple 2764, with "Mfd. by Apple" on label, three layout variations exist,
     1970 ....**5.00 - 10.00**

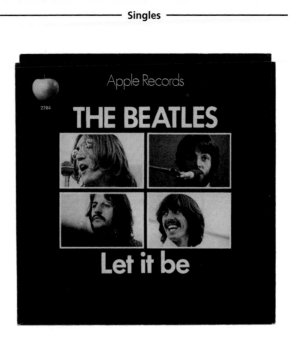

❑ Apple 2764, picture sleeve, all copies of the sleeve use "You Know My Name (Look Up The Number)" as the B-side title, 1970 (ILLUS.) ....**50.00 - 100.00**

- ❏ Apple 2764, with "All Rights Reserved" disclaimer, 1975 .... **10.00 - 20.00**
- ❏ Capitol 2764, orange label with "Capitol" at bottom, 1976 .... **3.00 - 6.00**
- ❏ Capitol 2764, purple label; notches along label's edge, 1978 .... **4.00 - 8.00**
- ❏ Capitol 2764, black label with colorband, 1983 .... **3.00 - 6.00**
- ❏ Capitol 2764, purple label; label has smooth edge,
  1988 .... **2.50 - 5.00**
- ❏ Capitol S7-17695, yellow vinyl, 1994 .... **2.00 - 4.00**

LET'S DANCE/IF YOU LOVE ME BABY

- ❏ Collectables 1521, despite label credit to The Beatles, A-side is a Tony Sheridan solo
  recording, 1987 .... **3.00 - 6.00**

LIKE DREAMERS DO/LOVE OF THE LOVED

- ❏ Backstage 1112, promotional 45 from "Oui" magazine, both songs are from the
  1962 Decca audition tapes, 1982 .... **12.50 - 25.00**

LIKE DREAMERS DO/THREE COOL CATS

- ❏ Backstage 1133, promotional picture disc, both songs are from the 1962 Decca
  audition tapes, 1983 .... **12.50 - 25.00**

THE LONG AND WINDING ROAD/FOR YOU BLUE

- ❏ Apple 2832, with small Capitol logo on bottom of B-side label,
  1970 .... **10.00 - 20.00**
- ❏ Apple 2832, With "Mfd. by Apple" on label, four layout variations exist,
  1970 .... **5.00 - 10.00**

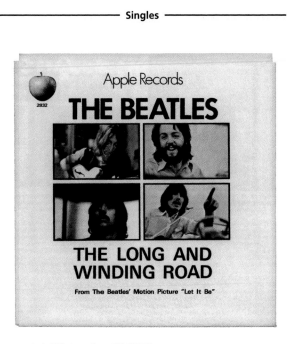

□   Apple 2832, picture sleeve, 1970 (ILLUS.) ....**50.00 - 100.00**

- ❏ Apple 2832, with "All Rights Reserved" disclaimer, 1975.................. **10.00 - 20.00**
- ❏ Capitol 2832, orange label with "Capitol" at bottom,
  1976..**3.00 - 6.00**
- ❏ Capitol 2832, purple label; notches along label's edge,
  1978..**4.00 - 8.00**
- ❏ Capitol 2832, black label with colorband, 1983...............................**3.00 - 6.00**
- ❏ Capitol 2832, purple label; label has smooth edge, 1988 ....**2.50 - 5.00**
- ❏ Capitol S7-18898, blue vinyl, 1996 ....**2.00 - 4.00**

LONG TALL SALLY/I REMEMBER YOU

❏　Collectables 1513, recorded live in Hamburg, 1982 ....**1.00 - 3.00**

❏　Collectables 1513, picture sleeve, 1982 ....**1.00 - 3.00**

LOVE ME DO (SAME ON BOTH SIDES)

❏　Capitol PB-5189, promo, orange and yellow swirl label,

　　1982 .... **7.50 - 15.00**

LOVE ME DO/P.S. I LOVE YOU

❏   Capitol 72076, orange and yellow swirl; Canadian release that was heavily
imported to the U.S.; it made the Billboard, Cash Box and Record World charts
with this catalog number before the Tollie single came out; this contains the first
released version of "Love Me Do," with Ringo Starr on drums and no tambourine,
which was not legally issued in the U.S. until 1980, 1963

(ILLUS.) ....**25.00 - 50.00**

❏ Tollie 9008, yellow label, black print, "TOLLIE" by itself with smaller "RECORDS" underneath, "T-9008" at 3 o'clock, 1964 .... **25.00 - 50.00**

❏ Tollie 9008, yellow label, black print, black "tollie" in thick box, two types styles exist, 1964 .... **25.00 - 50.00**

❏ Tollie 9008, yellow label, green print, green "tollie" in thick box, 1964 .... **25.00 - 50.00**

❏ Tollie 9008, yellow label, black print, thin black "TOLLIE" in thin box, 1964 .... **25.00 - 50.00**

❏ Tollie 9008, black label, silver print, thin silver "TOLLIE" in thin box, 1964 .... **30.00 - 60.00**

❏ Tollie 9008, yellow label, black print, "TOLLIE" in thin box, periods in "B.M.I." on both sides; this may be a counterfeit, 1964 .... **12.50 - 25.00**

- ❏ Tollie 9008, promo copy, white label, "TOLLIE" by itself with smaller "RECORDS" underneath, 1964 (ILLUS.) .... **200.00 - 400.00**
- ❏ Tollie 9008, promo copy, white label, black "tollie" in thick box, 1964... **200.00 - 400.00**

❏ Tollie 9008, picture sleeve, 1964 (ILLUS.) ....**75.00 - 150.00**
❏ Oldies 45 151, authentic copies have "Oldies 45" in white, counterfeits have "Oldies
45" in black, 1964 .... **7.50 - 15.00**

- Capitol Starline 6062, green swirl label, two type styles exist,
  1965 (ILLUS.) ....**60.00 - 120.00**
- Capitol B-5189, orange and yellow swirl label, black print,
  1982 ....**2.50 - 5.00**

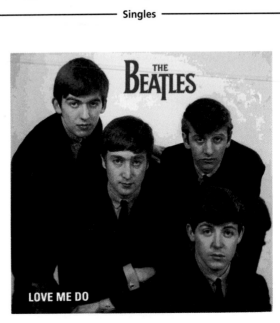

❏   Capitol B-5189, picture sleeve, 1982 (ILLUS.) ....**2.50 - 5.00**

❑ Capitol B-5189, black label with colorband, 1983 .... **3.00 - 6.00**

❑ Capitol B-5189, purple label, 1988 .... **2.00 - 4.00**

❑ Capitol S7-56785, red vinyl "error pressing," 1992 .... **15.00 - 30.00**

❑ Capitol S7-56785, black vinyl, 1992.. **2.00 - 4.00**

❑ Capitol 7PRO-79551/79552, promo only, 1992 .... **12.50 - 25.00**

❑ Capitol 7PRO-79551/79552, picture sleeve, 1992 .... **12.50 - 25.00**

LOVE OF THE LOVED/MEMPHIS

❑ Backstage 1122, promotional picture disc, both songs are from the 1962 Decca
audition tapes, 1983 .... **12.50 - 25.00**

LUCY IN THE SKY WITH DIAMONDS/WHEN I'M 64

❑ Capitol S7-18896, red vinyl, 1996 .... **2.00 - 4.00**

MAGICAL MYSTERY TOUR/HERE COMES THE SUN

❑ Capitol/Evatone 420827cs, Flexi-disc issued as giveaway by The Musicland Group;
"Musicland" version, 1982 .... **5.00 - 10.00**

❑ Capitol/Evatone 420827cs, Flexi-disc issued as giveaway by The Musicland Group;
"Discount" version, 1982.. **10.00 - 20.00**

❑ Capitol/Evatone 420827cs, Flexi-disc issued as giveaway by The Musicland Group;
"Sam Goody" version, 1982... **12.50 - 25.00**

MAGICAL MYSTERY TOUR/THE FOOL ON THE HILL

❑   Capitol S7-18890, yellow vinyl, 1996 (ILLUS.) ....**2.00 - 4.00**

MATCHBOX/SLOW DOWN

❏ Capitol 5255, orange and yellow swirl, without "A Subsidiary Of"... in perimeter
   label print, two type styles exist, 1964 .... **15.00 - 30.00**

❏ Capitol 5255, picture sleeve, straight cut or "tab cut" versions exist,
   1964 (ILLUS.) .... **75.00 - 150.00**

- ❏ Capitol 5255, orange and yellow swirl label with "A Subsidiary Of" in perimeter print, 1968...**25.00 - 50.00**
- ❏ Capitol 5255, red and orange "target" label with Capitol dome logo, 1969...**30.00 - 60.00**
- ❏ Capitol 5255, red and orange "target" label with Capitol round logo, 1969...**10.00 - 20.00**
- ❏ Apple 5255, with star on A-side label, "Slow Down" is labeled with the full apple, 1971...**15.00 - 30.00**
- ❏ Apple 5255, without star on A-side label, "Slow Down" is labeled with the full apple, 1971...**5.00 - 10.00**
- ❏ Apple 5255, with "All Rights Reserved" disclaimer, "Slow Down" is labeled with the full apple, 1975...**7.50 - 15.00**
- ❏ Capitol 5255, orange label with "Capitol" at bottom, 1976...**3.00 - 6.00**
- ❏ Capitol 5255, purple label, 1978...**7.50 - 15.00**
- ❏ Capitol Starline A-6284, blue label with "Stereo," 1981..................**4.00 - 8.00**
- ❏ Capitol Starline A-6284, blue label with "Mono," 1981...**12.50 - 25.00**
- ❏ Capitol Starline X-6284, blue label with "Mono," 1981 ....**2.50 - 5.00**
- ❏ Capitol Starline X-6284, black colorband label, 1986....................**3.00 - 6.00**
- ❏ Capitol Starline X-6284, purple label, 1988.................................**2.50 - 5.00**

MUSIC CITY/KFWBEATLES//YOU CAN'T DO THAT

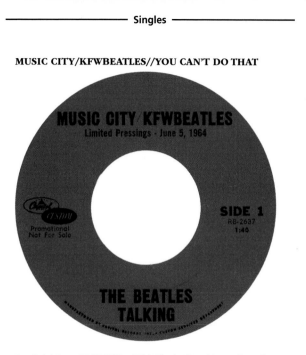

❏   Capitol Custom RB-2637/2638, red label, Side 1 has "Capitol Custom" logo, Side 2
    has "Capitol" logo, counterfeits have no Capitol logo on labels,
    1964 (ILLUS.) ....**500.00 – 1,000.**

❏ Capitol Custom RB-2637/2638, manila envelope with red print and 2 1/16-inch
flap, counterfeits have darker red print and 1 5/8-inch flap,
1964 (ILLUS.) ....**500.00 – 1,000.**

1964: SEASON'S GREETINGS FROM THE BEATLES

❏ Beatles Fan Club (1964), tri-fold soundcard, actually contains the 1963 Christmas
message, 1964 (ILLUS.) .... **150.00 - 300.00**

1966: SEASON'S GREETINGS FROM THE BEATLES

❏   Beatles Fan Club (1966), postcard, 1966 (ILLUS.)......................**75.00 - 150.00**

NORWEGIAN WOOD (THIS BIRD HAS FLOWN)/IF I NEEDED SOMEONE

❏   Capitol S7-18888, green vinyl; 1,000 pressed, given by Collectors' Choice Music to
    buyers of Beatles reissue LPs, 1995 ....**75.00 - 150.00**

❏   Capitol S7-19341, black vinyl, 1996 ....**1.00 - 3.00**

NOWHERE MAN/WHAT GOES ON

- ❏ Capitol 5587, orange and yellow swirl, without "A Subsidiary Of"... in perimeter label print; composers of "What Goes On" listed as "John Lennon-Paul McCartney," two type styles exist, 1966 (ILLUS.) .... **12.50 - 25.00**
- ❏ Capitol 5587, orange and yellow swirl, without "A Subsidiary Of"... in perimeter label print; composers of "What Goes On" listed as "Lennon-McCartney-Starkey," two type styles exist, 1966 .... **25.00 - 50.00**

❏ Capitol 5587, picture sleeve, straight cut and "tab-cut" versions exist,
1966 (ILLUS.) .... **20.00 - 40.00**

- ❏ Capitol 5587, orange and yellow swirl label with "A Subsidiary Of" in perimeter print, three type styles exist, 1968..**25.00 - 50.00**
- ❏ Capitol 5587, red and orange "target" label with Capitol dome logo, 1969..**30.00 - 60.00**
- ❏ Capitol 5587, red and orange "target" label with Capitol round logo, 1969..**10.00 - 20.00**
- ❏ Apple 5587, with star on A-side label, 1971 ....**15.00 - 30.00**
- ❏ Apple 5587, without star on A-side label, 1971 ....**5.00 - 10.00**
- ❏ Apple 5587, with "All Rights Reserved" disclaimer, 1975..................**7.50 - 15.00**
- ❏ Capitol 5587, orange label with "Capitol" at bottom, 1976 ....**3.00 - 6.00**
- ❏ Capitol 5587, purple label, 1978...**7.50 - 15.00**
- ❏ Capitol Starline A-6294, blue label with "Stereo," 1981.....................**4.00 - 8.00**
- ❏ Capitol Starline A-6294, blue label with "Mono," 1981 ....**12.50 - 25.00**
- ❏ Capitol Starline X-6294, blue label with "Mono," 1981 ....**2.50 - 5.00**
- ❏ Capitol Starline X-6294, black colorband label, 1986........................**3.00 - 6.00**
- ❏ Capitol Starline X-6294, purple label, 1988......................................**2.50 - 5.00**
- ❏ Capitol S7-18894, green vinyl, 1996 ....**2.00 - 4.00**

OB-LA-DI, OB-LA-DA (MONO/STEREO)

❏ Capitol P-4347, promo, white label, 1976 ....**20.00 - 40.00**

OB-LA-DI, OB-LA-DA/JULIA

❏ Capitol 4347, orange label with "Capitol" at bottom, 1976 ....**4.00 - 8.00**
❏ Capitol 4347, picture sleeve, sleeves are individually numbered; very low numbers (under 1000) can fetch premium prices, 1976..................................**4.00 - 8.00**
❏ Capitol 4347, purple label; notches along label's edge, 1978 ....**4.00 - 8.00**
❏ Capitol 4347, black label with colorband, 1983..................................**3.00 - 6.00**
❏ Capitol 4347, purple label; label has smooth edge, 1988 ....**2.50 - 5.00**

❏ Capitol S7-18900, clear vinyl, 1996 (ILLUS.) ....**2.00 - 4.00**

PAPERBACK WRITER/RAIN

❏   Capitol 5651, orange and yellow swirl, without "A Subsidiary Of"... in perimeter

     label print, two type styles exist, 1966 .... **12.50 - 25.00**

❏   Capitol 5651, picture sleeve, straight cut and "tab-cut" versions exist,

     1966 (ILLUS.) .... **37.50 - 75.00**

- ❏ Capitol 5651, orange and yellow swirl with "A Subsidiary Of"... on perimeter print in white, two type styles exist, 1968...**25.00 - 50.00**
- ❏ Capitol 5651, orange and yellow swirl with "A Subsidiary Of"... on perimeter print in black, 1968...**50.00 - 100.00**
- ❏ Capitol 5651, red and orange "target" label with Capitol dome logo, 1969...**30.00 - 60.00**
- ❏ Capitol 5651, red and orange "target" label with Capitol round logo, 1969...**10.00 - 20.00**
- ❏ Apple 5651, with star on A-side label, 1971 ....**15.00 - 30.00**
- ❏ Apple 5651, without star on A-side label, 1971 ....**5.00 - 10.00**
- ❏ Apple 5651, with "All Rights Reserved" disclaimer, 1975...................**7.50 - 15.00**
- ❏ Capitol 5651, orange label with "Capitol" at bottom, 1976 ....**3.00 - 6.00**
- ❏ Capitol 5651, purple label, 1978...**7.50 - 15.00**
- ❏ Capitol Starline A-6296, blue label with "Stereo," 1981 ....**4.00 - 8.00**
- ❏ Capitol Starline A-6296, blue label with "Mono," 1981 ....**12.50 - 25.00**
- ❏ Capitol Starline X-6296, blue label with "Mono," 1981 ....**2.50 - 5.00**
- ❏ Capitol Starline X-6296, black colorband label, 1986.......................**3.00 - 6.00**
- ❏ Capitol Starline X-6296, purple label, 1988....................................**2.50 - 5.00**
- ❏ Capitol S7-18902, red vinyl, 1996 ....**2.00 - 4.00**

PENNY LANE/STRAWBERRY FIELDS FOREVER

❑   Capitol 5810, orange and yellow swirl, without "A Subsidiary Of"... in perimeter
label print; "Penny Lane" time listed as 3:00, two type styles exist,
1967 (ILLUS.) .... **12.50 - 25.00**

❏ Capitol 5810, orange and yellow swirl, without "A Subsidiary Of"... in perimeter label print; "Penny Lane" time listed as 2:57, two type styles exist, 1967 (ILLUS.) ....**15.00 - 30.00**

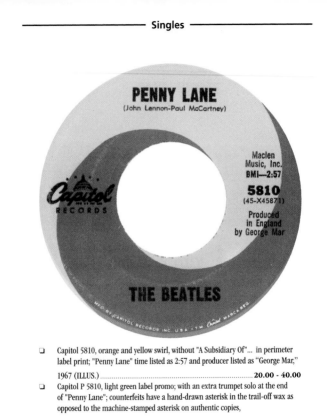

❑   Capitol 5810, orange and yellow swirl, without "A Subsidiary Of"... in perimeter
    label print; "Penny Lane" time listed as 2:57 and producer listed as "George Mar,"
    1967 (ILLUS.) .... **20.00 - 40.00**
❑   Capitol P 5810, light green label promo; with an extra trumpet solo at the end
    of "Penny Lane"; counterfeits have a hand-drawn asterisk in the trail-off wax as
    opposed to the machine-stamped asterisk on authentic copies,
    1967 .... **150.00 - 300.00**

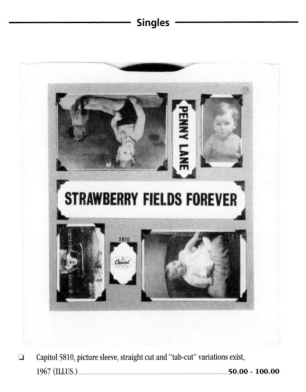

❑   Capitol 5810, picture sleeve, straight cut and "tab-cut" variations exist,
     1967 (ILLUS.) ....**50.00 - 100.00**

- Capitol 5810, orange and yellow swirl label with "A Subsidiary Of" in perimeter print, 1968..**25.00 - 50.00**
- Capitol 5810, red and orange "target" label with Capitol dome logo, 1969...**30.00 - 60.00**
- Capitol 5810, red and orange "target" label with Capitol round logo, 1969...**10.00 - 20.00**
- Apple 5810, with star on A-side label, "Strawberry Fields Forever" is labeled with the full apple, 1971...**15.00 - 30.00**
- Apple 5810, without star on A-side label, "Strawberry Fields Forever" is labeled with the full apple, 1971...**5.00 - 10.00**
- Apple 5810, with "All Rights Reserved" disclaimer, "Strawberry Fields Forever" is labeled with the full apple, 1975 ....**7.50 - 15.00**
- Capitol 5810, orange label with "Capitol" at bottom, 1976 ....**3.00 - 6.00**
- Capitol 5810, purple label, 1978..**7.50 - 15.00**
- Capitol Starline A-6299, blue label with "Stereo," 1981......................**4.00 - 8.00**
- Capitol Starline A-6299, blue label with "Mono," 1981 ....**12.50 - 25.00**
- Capitol Starline X-6299, blue label with "Mono," 1981 ....**3.00 - 6.00**
- Capitol Starline X-6299, black colorband label, 1986......................**3.00 - 6.00**
- Capitol Starline X-6299, purple label, 1988..................................**2.50 - 5.00**
- Capitol S7-17697, red vinyl, "Strawberry Fields Forever" listed as A-side, 1994..**2.00 - 4.00**

PLEASE PLEASE ME/ASK ME WHY

(NOTE: This record was not issued with a picture sleeve; bootleg picture
sleeves exist.)

❏ Vee Jay 498, group's name misspelled "The Beattles"; number is "VJ 498", both vinyl
and styrene versions of this record exist, 1963 (ILLUS.) .... **1,000. – 1.500.**
❏ Vee Jay 498, group's name misspelled "The Beattles"; number is "#498",
1963 ....**1,100. – 1,600.**

- ❏ Vee Jay 498, Correct spelling; number is "VJ 498"; thick print,
  1963 (ILLUS.) .... **600.00 - 900.00**
- ❏ Vee Jay 498, Correct spelling; number is "#498", 1963 .... **1,100. – 1,600.**
- ❏ Vee Jay 498, Correct spelling; number is "VJ 498"; brackets label, limited repressing,
  1964 .... **1,500. – 2,000.**
- ❏ Vee Jay 498, one side has an oval label with "The Beatles," the other has a brackets
  label with "The Beatles,", 1964 .... **2,250. – 3,000.**
- ❏ Vee Jay 498, white label promo, misspelled "The Beattles",
  1963 .... **550.00 – 1,100.**

PLEASE PLEASE ME/FROM ME TO YOU

❑   Vee Jay 581, black rainbow label, oval logo, five type styles exist,
1964 (ILLUS.) .... **25.00 - 50.00**

❑ Vee Jay 581, black rainbow label, brackets logo, three type styles exist,
1964..**30.00 - 60.00**

❑ Vee Jay 581, plain black label, oval logo, 1964 ....**30.00 - 60.00**

❑ Vee Jay 581, plain black label, brackets logo, no horizontal lines; two type styles
exist, 1964 ....**37.50 - 75.00**

❑ Vee Jay 581, plain black label, brackets logo, with two horizontal lines through
center hole, 1964 ....**22.50 - 45.00**

❑ Vee Jay 581, plain black label, "VEE JAY" stands alone, 1964...........**30.00 - 60.00**

❑ Vee Jay 581, plain black label, "VJ" by itself with "VEE JAY RECORDS" under it in
small type, 1964..**32.50 - 65.00**

❑ Vee Jay 581, yellow label, 1964 ....**37.50 - 75.00**

❑ Vee Jay 581, white label, not a promo, 1964 ....**80.00 - 160.00**

❑ Capitol Starline 6063, green swirl label, two type styles exist,
1965 ....**60.00 - 120.00**

❏ Vee Jay 581, purple label, 1964 (ILLUS.) .... **125.00 - 250.00**
❏ Vee Jay 581, white label, blue and black print; "Promotional Copy" on label,
   1964 .... **400.00 - 600.00**

❏ Vee Jay 581, picture sleeve, legitimate sleeves have "The Beatles" in red, counterfeits have "The Beatles" in other colors,

1964 (ILLUS.) .... **250.00 - 500.00**

THE RECORD THAT STARTED "BEATLEMANIA"

ENGLAND'S SENSATIONS

JUST DID
JACK PAAR SHOW
(JAN. 3)

COMING UP
ED SULLIVAN
(FEB. 9 & FEB. 16)

FEATURED IN TIME, LIFE,
NEWSWEEK

THIS IS THE RECORD
THAT STARTED IT ALL

PLEASE, PLEASE ME
AND
FROM ME TO YOU
BY
THE BEATLES

[VJ]
VEE-JAY
RECORDS

VJ-581

(PROMOTION COPY)

❑ Vee Jay 581, picture sleeve, special "The Record That Started Beatlemania" promo-
only sleeve, 1964 (ILLUS.) .... **1,750. – 2,500.**
❑ Oldies 45 150, authentic copies have "Oldies 45" in white print, fakes have "Oldies
45" in black, 1964 .... **7.50 - 15.00**

REAL LOVE/BABY'S IN BLACK (LIVE)

❏   Apple 58544, small center hole, 1996...............................**1.00 - 3.00**

❏   Apple 58544, picture sleeve, 1996 (ILLUS.) ....**1.00 - 3.00**

RED SAILS IN THE SUNSET/MATCHBOX

❏ Collectables 1511, recorded live in Hamburg, 1982 ....**1.00 - 3.00**

❏ Collectables 1511, picture sleeve, 1982 ....**1.00 - 3.00**

ROCKY RACCOON/WHY DON'T WE DO IT IN THE ROAD?

❏ Capitol/Evatone 420828cs, Flexi-disc issued as giveaway by The Musicland Group;
"Musicland" version, 1982 ....**5.00 - 10.00**

❏ Capitol/Evatone 420828cs, Flexi-disc issued as giveaway by The Musicland Group;
"Discount" version, 1982...**10.00 - 20.00**

❏ Capitol/Evatone 420828cs, Flexi-disc issued as giveaway by The Musicland Group;
"Sam Goody" version, 1982..**12.50 - 25.00**

ROLL OVER BEETHOVEN/MISERY

- ❏ Capitol Starline 6065, green swirl label, two type styles exist,
  1965 (ILLUS.) ....**60.00 - 120.00**
- ❏ Capitol 6065, red and orange "target" label, 1971 ....**15.00 - 30.00**

ROLL OVER BEETHOVEN/PLEASE MISTER POSTMAN

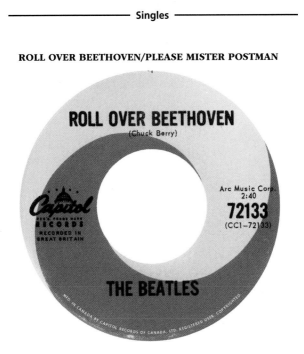

❏ Capitol 72133, orange and yellow swirl; Canadian release that was heavily
  imported to the U.S., 1964 (ILLUS.).. **25.00 - 50.00**

RUBY BABY/YA YA

❑ Collectables 1523, despite label credit to The Beatles, both are by Tony Sheridan
without the Fab Four, 1987 ....**3.00 - 6.00**

SGT. PEPPER'S LONELY HEARTS CLUB BAND-WITH A LITTLE HELP FROM MY FRIENDS (MONO/STEREO)

❑ Capitol P-4612, promo, white label, 1978 ....**20.00 - 40.00**

SGT. PEPPER'S LONELY HEARTS CLUB BAND-WITH A LITTLE HELP FROM MY FRIENDS/A DAY IN THE LIFE

❑ Capitol 4612, purple label; notches along label's edge,
1978 ....**4.00 - 8.00**

❑ Capitol 4612, picture sleeve, 1978 ....**10.00 - 20.00**

❑ Capitol 4612, black label with colorband, 1983 ....**3.00 - 6.00**

❑ Capitol 4612, purple label; label has smooth edge, 1988 ....**2.50 - 5.00**

❑ Capitol S7-17701, clear vinyl, 1994 ....**2.00 - 4.00**

SHE LOVES YOU/I'LL GET YOU

❏   Swan 4152, white label, red print; no "Don't Drop Out" on label; no quotes around
song titles, 1963 (ILLUS.) .... **300.00 - 600.00**

❑ Swan 4152, white label, red print; no "Don't Drop Out" on label, quotes around song titles; authentic copies have "Gil Music" on one line and "Corp. BMI" underneath, 1963 .... **325.00 - 650.00**

❑ Swan 4152, white label, red print,;"Don't Drop Out" on label; no quotes around song titles, 1963 .... **325.00 - 650.00**

❑ Swan 4152, counterfeit; white label, red or maroon print, no "Don't Drop Out" on label, quotes around song titles; smaller numbers in trailoff area, late 1960s .... **4.00 - 8.00**

❑ Swan 4152, promo, white label, black print, no "Don't Drop Out" on label, with "A" added to print on "She Loves You" side, 1963 .... **250.00 - 500.00**

❑ Swan 4152, promo, white label, black print, no "Don't Drop Out" on label, with two "X"'s added to print on "She Loves You" side, 1963 .... **250.00 - 500.00**

❑ Swan 4152, promo, white label, black print, "Don't Drop Out" on label, with single "X" added to print on "She Loves You" side, 1964 .... **225.00 - 450.00**

- ❏ Swan 4152, white label, blue print, 1964 (ILLUS.) .... **300.00 - 600.00**
- ❏ Swan 4152, black label, silver print, no "Don't Drop Out" on label,
  1964.. **20.00 - 40.00**

❏ Swan 4152, black label, silver print, "Don't Drop Out" on label, 1964 .... **15.00 - 30.00**

❏ Swan 4152, black label, silver print, "Produced by George Martin" on both labels, 1964 .... **25.00 - 50.00**

❏ Swan 4152, black label, silver print, "Produced by George Martin" on only one label, 1964 .... **25.00 - 50.00**

❏ Swan 4152, counterfeit, black label, silver print, no "Don't Drop Out" on label, smaller numbers in trailoff area, this looks like the white label counterfeit shown earlier except with everything in black and silver rather than white and red/maroon, late 1960s .... **4.00 - 8.00**

- [ ] Swan 4152, picture sleeve, 1964 (ILLUS.) ....**60.00 - 120.00**
- [ ] Capitol S7-17688, red vinyl, 1994 ....**2.00 - 4.00**

SHE'S NOT THE ONLY GIRL IN TOWN/MORE THAN I NEED MYSELF

- [ ] Collectables 1517, despite label credit to The Beatles, both are Peter Best recordings, 1987 ....**5.00 - 10.00**

SIE LIEBT DICH (SHE LOVES YOU)/I'LL GET YOU

❑ Swan 4182, white label, "Sie Liebt Dich (She Loves You)" on one line,
1964 (ILLUS.) ....75.00 - 150.00

❏ Swan 4182, white label, "(She Loves You)" under "Sie Liebt Dich," wide red print,
1964..**75.00 - 150.00**
❏ Swan 4182, white label, "(She Loves You)" under "Sie Liebt Dich," narrow print,
1964..**75.00 - 150.00**
❏ Swan 4182, white label, "(She Loves You)" under "Sie Liebt Dich," wide orange
print, 1964..**87.50 - 175.00**
❏ Swan 4182, promo, white label, black print, "Sie Liebt Dich (She Loves You)" on
one line, 1964..**225.00 - 450.00**
❏ Swan 4182, promo, white label, black print, "(She Loves You)" under "Sie Liebt
Dich", 1964 ....**200.00 - 400.00**

SLOW DOWN/MATCHBOX
See MATCHBOX/SLOW DOWN.

SOMETHING/COME TOGETHER

❏ Apple 2654, With "Mfd. by Apple" on label, 1969 .... **5.00 - 10.00**

❏ Apple 2654, with small Capitol logo on bottom of B-side label,
1969 (ILLUS.) ....**50.00 - 100.00**

- ❏ Apple 2654, With "All Rights Reserved" disclaimer, 1975 .... **10.00 - 20.00**
- ❏ Capitol 2654, orange label with "Capitol" at bottom, 1976 .... **3.00 - 6.00**
- ❏ Capitol 2654, purple label; notches along label's edge, 1978 .... **3.00 - 6.00**
- ❏ Capitol 2654, black label with colorband, 1983 .... **3.00 - 6.00**
- ❏ Capitol 2654, purple label; label has smooth edge, 1988 .... **2.50 - 5.00**
- ❏ Capitol S7-17698, blue vinyl, 1994 .... **2.00 - 4.00**

STRAWBERRY FIELDS FOREVER/PENNY LANE

See PENNY LANE/STRAWBERRY FIELDS FOREVER.

SWEET GEORGIA BROWN/TAKE OUT SOME INSURANCE ON ME BABY

- ❏ Atco 6302, white and yellow label, no songwriting credit on B-side,
  1964 .... **100.00 - 200.00**
- ❏ Atco 6302, white and yellow label, with "Singleton-Hall" songwriting credit on
  B-side, 1964 .... **100.00 - 200.00**
- ❏ Atco 6302, promo, all-white label, no songwriting credit on B-side,
  1964 .... **100.00 - 200.00**
- ❏ Atco 6302, promo, all-white label, with "Singleton-Hall" songwriting credit on
  B-side, 1964 .... **100.00 - 200.00**

TALKIN' BOUT YOU/SHIMMY SHAKE

- ❏ Collectables 1512, recorded live in Hamburg,1982 .... **1.00 - 3.00**
- ❏ Collectables 1512, picture sleeve, 1982 .... **1.00 - 3.00**

A TASTE OF HONEY/BESAME MUCHO

- ❏ Collectables 1505, recorded live in Hamburg,1982 .... **1.00 - 3.00**
- ❏ Collectables 1505, picture sleeve, 1982 .... **1.00 - 3.00**

TICKET TO RIDE/YES IT IS

(On every copy of this 45 through the 1976 release, both
sides made the claim, "From the United Artists
Release 'Eight Arms to Hold You'." There is nothing
collectible to be implied because the record has the
wrong movie title on it.)

❑   Capitol 5407, orange and yellow swirl, without "A Subsidiary Of"... in perimeter
      label print, three type styles exist, 1965..**15.00 - 30.00**

❑   Capitol 5407, picture sleeve, straight cut and "tab-cut" versions exist,
      1965 (ILLUS.) ....**50.00 - 100.00**

❏ Capitol 5407, orange and yellow swirl with "A Subsidiary Of"... on perimeter print
in white, two type styles exist, 1968..**25.00 - 50.00**

❏ Capitol 5407, orange and yellow swirl with "A Subsidiary Of"... on perimeter print
in black, 1968..**50.00 - 100.00**

❏ Capitol 5407, red and orange "target" label with Capitol dome logo,
1969..**30.00 - 60.00**

❏ Capitol 5407, red and orange "target" label with Capitol round logo,
1969..**10.00 - 20.00**

❏ Apple 5407, with star on A-side label, 1971..**15.00 - 30.00**

❏ Apple 5407, without star on A-side label, 1971..**5.00 - 10.00**

❏ Apple 5407, with "All Rights Reserved" disclaimer, 1975..**7.50 - 15.00**

❏ Capitol 5407, orange label with "Capitol" at bottom, 1976..**3.00 - 6.00**

❏ Capitol 5407, purple label, 1978..**7.50 - 15.00**

❏ Capitol Starline A-6288, blue label with "Stereo," 1981..**4.00 - 8.00**

❏ Capitol Starline A-6288, blue label with "Mono," 1981..**12.50 - 25.00**

❏ Capitol Starline X-6288, blue label with "Mono," 1981..**3.00 - 6.00**

❏ Capitol Starline X-6288, black colorband label, 1986..**3.00 - 6.00**

❏ Capitol Starline X-6288, purple label, 1988..**2.50 - 5.00**

TILL THERE WAS YOU/EVERYBODY'S TRYING TO BE MY BABY

❏ Collectables 1506, recorded live in Hamburg, 1982..**1.00 - 3.00**

❏ Collectables 1506, picture sleeve, 1982..**1.00 - 3.00**

TILL THERE WAS YOU/THREE COOL CATS (BOTH ON SAME SIDE)

❏ Eva-Tone 830771X. red plastic flexidisc; issued as giveaway with a Beatles price
guide, 1983..**3.00 - 6.00**

TO KNOW HER IS TO LOVE HER/LITTLE QUEENIE

❏   Collectables 1508, recorded live in Hamburg, 1982.............................**1.00 - 3.00**

❏   Collectables 1508, picture sleeve, 1982 ....**1.00 - 3.00**

TWIST AND SHOUT (STEREO/STEREO)

❏   Capitol P-B-5624, promo, white label, 1986....................................**7.50 - 15.00**

TWIST AND SHOUT/THERE'S A PLACE

(NOTE: Tollie 9001 was not issued with a picture sleeve, though bootleg
    picture sleeves exist.)

- ❏ Tollie 9001, yellow label, black print, "TOLLIE" by itself with smaller "RECORDS"
    underneath, "9001" at 3 o'clock, 1964 (ILLUS.) .... **25.00 - 50.00**
- ❏ Tollie 9001, yellow label, green print, "TOLLIE" by itself with smaller "RECORDS"
    underneath, 1964 .... **40.00 - 80.00**

❏ Tollie 9001, yellow label, black print, black "tollie" in thick box, 1964 .... **25.00 - 50.00**

❏ Tollie 9001, yellow label, purple print, purple "tollie" in thick box, "#9001" at 9 o'clock, 1964 .... **40.00 - 80.00**

❏ Tollie 9001, yellow label, black print, purple "tollie" in thick box, four type styles exist, 1964 .... **30.00 - 60.00**

❏ Tollie 9001, yellow label, green print, green "tollie" in thick box, 1964 .... **25.00 - 50.00**

❏ Tollie 9001, yellow label, blue print, "TOLLIE" in brackets, 1964 .... **30.00 - 60.00**

❏ Tollie 9001, yellow label, black print, "TOLLIE" in brackets, 1964 .... **37.50 - 75.00**

❏ Tollie 9001, yellow label, black print, thin black "TOLLIE" in thin box, 1964 .... **25.00 - 50.00**

- [ ] Tollie 9001, black label, silver print, thin silver "TOLLIE" in thin box,
  1964 (ILLUS.) ....**30.00 - 60.00**
- [ ] Tollie 9001, yellow label, black print, "TOLLIE" in thin box, periods in "B.M.I." on
  A-side; this may be a counterfeit, 1964 ....**12.50 - 25.00**
- [ ] Oldies 45 152, authentic copies have "Oldies 45" in white print, fakes have "Oldies
  45" in black, 1964 ....**7.50 - 15.00**

THERE'S A PLACE
(John Lennon-Paul McCartney)

Gil Music
Corp.
BMI-1:48
6061
(45-X45017)
Recorded
in England

THE STAR LINE

THE BEATLES

MFD. BY CAPITOL RECORDS, INC., U.S.A. • T.M. *Capitol* MARCA REG.

❏ Capitol Starline 6061, green swirl label, two type styles exist,
1965 (ILLUS.) ....**60.00 - 120.00**

❏ Capitol B-5624, black label with colorband, 1986 ....**2.50 - 5.00**

❏ Capitol B-5624, purple label, 1988 ....**2.50 - 5.00**

❏ Capitol S7-17699, pink vinyl, 1994 ....**2.00 - 4.00**

WE CAN WORK IT OUT/DAY TRIPPER

❑ Capitol 5555, orange and yellow swirl, without "A Subsidiary Of"... in perimeter label print, no times listed on either label, two type styles exist, 1965 (ILLUS.) ....**25.00 - 50.00**

❑ Capitol 5555, orange and yellow swirl, without "A Subsidiary Of"... in perimeter label print, with times filled in, two type styles exist,1965..............**15.00 - 30.00**

- ❏ Capitol 5555, picture sleeve, straight cut and "tab-cut" versions exist,
  1965 (ILLUS.) ....**30.00 - 60.00**
- ❏ Capitol 5555, orange and yellow swirl label with "A Subsidiary Of" in perimeter
  print in white, two type styles exist, 1968 ....**25.00 - 50.00**
- ❏ Capitol 5555, orange and yellow swirl label with "A Subsidiary Of" in perimeter
  print in black, 1968 ....**25.00 - 100.00**

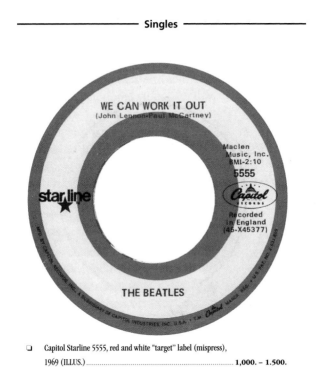

❏ Capitol Starline 5555, red and white "target" label (mispress),
   1969 (ILLUS.) .... **1,000. – 1.500.**

- ❏ Capitol 5555, red and orange "target" label with Capitol dome logo, 1969 ....**30.00 - 60.00**
- ❏ Capitol 5555, red and orange "target" label with Capitol round logo, 1969 ....**10.00 - 20.00**
- ❏ Apple 5555, with star on A-side label, 1971 ....**15.00 - 30.00**
- ❏ Apple 5555, without star on A-side label, 1971 ....**5.00 - 10.00**
- ❏ Apple 5555, with "All Rights Reserved" disclaimer, 1975 ....**7.50 - 15.00**
- ❏ Capitol 5555, orange label with "Capitol" at bottom, 1976 ....**3.00 - 6.00**
- ❏ Capitol 5555, purple label, 1978 ....**7.50 - 15.00**
- ❏ Capitol Starline A-6293, blue label with "Stereo," 1981 ....**4.00 - 8.00**
- ❏ Capitol Starline A-6293, blue label with "Mono," 1981 ....**12.50 - 25.00**
- ❏ Capitol Starline X-6293, blue label with "Mono," 1981 ....**3.00 - 6.00**
- ❏ Capitol Starline X-6293, black colorband label, 1986 ....**3.00 - 6.00**
- ❏ Capitol Starline X-6293, purple label, 1988.....................................**2.50 - 5.00**
- ❏ Capitol S7-18895, pink vinyl, 1996 ....**2.00 - 4.00**

WE WISH YOU A MERRY CHRISTMAS AND A HAPPY NEW YEAR

❏ Vee Jay (no #), picture sleeve, used with any Vee Jay-related Beatles single in 1964-65 holiday season; most frequently found with records on the "Oldies 45" label, 1964 (ILLUS.) ....**40.00 - 80.00**

WHAT'D I SAY/SWEET GEORGIA BROWN

❏   Collectables 1522, Despite label credit to The Beatles, A-side is a Tony Sheridan solo recording, 1987 ....**3.00 - 6.00**

WHERE HAVE YOU BEEN ALL MY LIFE/MR. MOONLIGHT

❏   Collectables 1504, recorded live in Hamburg,1982 ....**1.00 - 3.00**

❏   Collectables 1504, picture sleeve, 1982 ....**1.00 - 3.00**

WHILE MY GUITAR GENTLY WEEPS/BLACKBIRD

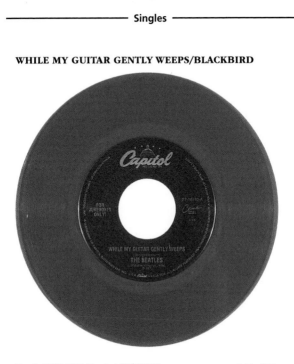

❏　Capitol S7-18892, blue vinyl, 1996 (ILLUS.) ....**2.00 - 4.00**

WHY/CRY FOR A SHADOW

❏ MGM K13227, by "The Beatles with Tony Sheridan," black label,
  1964 ....**75.00 - 150.00**
❏ MGM K13227, by "The Beatles with Tony Sheridan," yellow label "Special Disc
  Jockey Record," 1964 ....**125.00 - 250.00**

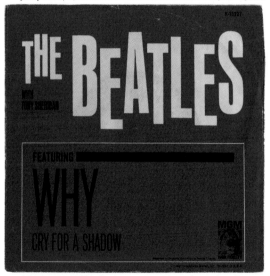

❏ MGM K13227, by "The Beatles with Tony Sheridan," picture sleeve
  1964 (ILLUS.) ....**200.00 - 400.00**

WHY/I'LL TRY ANYWAY

❑ Collectables 1524, despite label credit to The Beatles, B-side is a Peter Best
recording, 1987 ....**3.00 - 6.00**

YELLOW SUBMARINE/ELEANOR RIGBY

❑ Capitol 5715, orange and yellow swirl, without "A Subsidiary Of"... in perimeter
label print; perimeter print is white, three type styles exist, 1966 .... **12.50 - 25.00**

❑ Capitol 5715, orange and yellow swirl, without "A Subsidiary Of"... in perimeter
label print; perimeter print is yellow on both sides, 1966
(ILLUS.) ....**25.00 - 50.00**

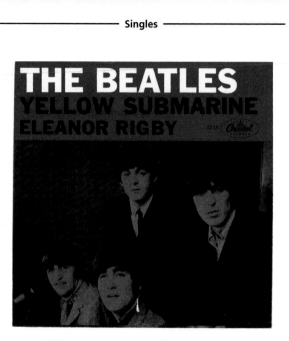

❏　Capitol 5715, picture sleeve, straight cut and "tab-cut" versions exist,
1966 (ILLUS.) ....**50.00 - 100.00**

❏ Capitol 5715, orange and yellow swirl label with "A Subsidiary Of" in perimeter print, two type styles exist, 1968 ....**25.00 - 50.00**

❏ Capitol/Americom 5715, four-inch flexi-disc sold in vending machines, translucent blue, 1969 ....**1,500. – 2,000.**

❏ Capitol 5715, red and orange "target" label with Capitol round logo, 1969 ....**30.00 - 60.00**

❏ Capitol 5715, red and orange "target" label with Capitol dome logo, 1969 ....**10.00 - 20.00**

❏ Apple 5715, with star on A-side label, 1971 ....**15.00 - 30.00**

❏ Apple 5715, without star on A-side label, 1971 ....**5.00 - 10.00**

❏ Apple 5715, with "All Rights Reserved" disclaimer, 1975 ....**7.50 - 15.00**

❏ Capitol 5715, orange label with "Capitol" at bottom, 1976 ....**3.00 - 6.00**

❏ Capitol 5715, purple label, 1978 ....**7.50 - 15.00**

❏ Capitol Starline A-6297, blue label with "Stereo," 1981 ....**4.00 - 8.00**

❏ Capitol Starline A-6297, blue label with "Mono," 1981 ....**12.50 - 25.00**

❏ Capitol Starline X-6297, blue label with "Mono," 1981 ....**3.00 - 6.00**

❏ Capitol Starline X-6297, black colorband label, 1986 ....**3.00 - 6.00**

❏ Capitol Starline X-6297, purple label, 1988 ....**2.50 - 5.00**

❏ Capitol S7-17696, yellow vinyl, 1994 ....**2.00 - 4.00**

YESTERDAY/ACT NATURALLY

❏ Capitol 5498, orange and yellow swirl, without "A Subsidiary Of"... in perimeter

   label print, two type styles exist, 1965 ....**15.00 - 30.00**

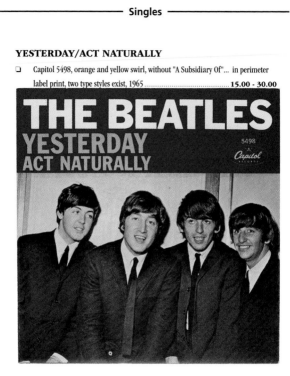

❏ Capitol 5498, picture sleeve, straight cut and "tab-cut" versions exist,

   1965 (ILLUS.) ....**50.00 - 100.00**

❑ Capitol 5498, orange and yellow swirl with "A Subsidiary Of"... on perimeter print in white, three type styles exist, 1968 .... **25.00 - 50.00**

❑ Capitol 5498, orange and yellow swirl with "A Subsidiary Of"... on perimeter print in black, 1968 .... **50.00 - 100.00**

❑ Capitol 5498, red and orange "target" label with Capitol dome logo, 1969 .... **30.00 - 60.00**

❑ Capitol 5498, red and orange "target" label with Capitol round logo, 1969 .... **10.00 - 20.00**

❑ Apple 5498, with star on A-side label, "Act Naturally" is labeled with the full apple, 1971 .... **15.00 - 30.00**

❑ Apple 5498, without star on A-side label, "Act Naturally" is labeled with the full apple, 1971 .... **5.00 - 10.00**

❑ Apple 5498, with "All Rights Reserved" disclaimer, "Act Naturally" is labeled with the full apple, 1975 .... **7.50 - 15.00**

❑ Capitol 5498, orange label with "Capitol" at bottom, 1976 .... **3.00 - 6.00**

❑ Capitol 5498, purple label, 1978 .... **7.50 - 15.00**

❑ Capitol Starline A-6291, blue label with "Stereo," 1981 .... **4.00 - 8.00**

❑ Capitol Starline A-6291, blue label with "Mono," 1981 .... **12.50 - 25.00**

❑ Capitol Starline X-6291, blue label with "Mono," 1981 .... **3.00 - 6.00**

❑ Capitol Starline X-6291, black colorband label, 1986 .... **2.50 - 5.00**

❑ Capitol Starline X-6291, purple label, 1988 .... **3.00 - 6.00**

❑ Capitol S7-18901, pink vinyl, 1996 .... **2.00 - 4.00**

**YOU'VE GOT TO HIDE YOUR LOVE AWAY/I'VE JUST
SEEN A FACE**

❏   Capitol S7-18889, gold/orange vinyl, 1996 (ILLUS.) ....**2.00 - 4.00**

7-Inch Extended Plays

BABY IT'S YOU

(Contents: Baby It's You/I'll Follow the Sun//Devil in Her
   Heart/Boys)

❑   Apple 58348, all from BBC sessions, 1995 ....**2.00 - 4.00**

❑   Apple 58348, picture sleeve, 1995 (ILLUS.) ....**2.00 - 4.00**

BACKBEAT

(Contents: Ain't She Sweet/Cry for a Shadow//My Bonnie/
The Saints)

❏   Polydor PRO 1113-7, promo only, 1994 .... **12.50 - 25.00**

❏   Polydor PRO 1113-7, picture sleeve, 1994 .... **12.50 - 25.00**

THE BEATLES' SECOND ALBUM

(Contents: Thank You Girl/Devil in Her Heart/Money
(That's What I Want)//Long Tall Sally/I Call Your
Name/Please Mister Postman

❏ Capitol SXA-2080, stereo jukebox edition, small hole, plays at 33 1/3 rpm, 1964
(ILLUS.) .... **200.00 - 400.00**

❏ Capitol SXA-2080, picture sleeve, with five jukebox title strips and three miniature covers intact; deduct 33 percent if the strips and covers are missing, deduct less if material is there but not intact, 1964 (ILLUS.) ....300.00 - 600.00

THE BEATLES' SECOND OPEN-END INTERVIEW

(Contents: Interview/Roll Over Beethoven//Please Mr.
   Postman/Thank You Girl)

❑   Capitol PRO-2598/2599, promo only, black colorband label, small hole, plays at 33
   1/3 rpm, 1964 (ILLUS.) .... **400.00 - 800.00**

❏ Capitol PRO-2598/2599, picture sleeve, contains script for interview on one side, 1964 (ILLUS.) .... **500.00 – 1,000.**

FOUR BY THE BEATLES

(Contents: Roll Over Beethoven/This Boy//All My Loving/
Please Mister Postman)

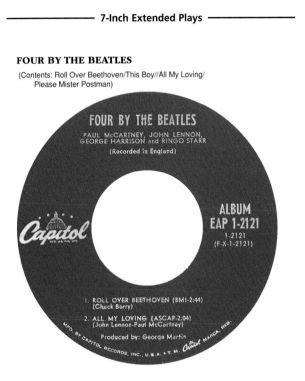

□ Capitol EAP 1-2121, turquoise label, 1964 (ILLUS.) .... **50.00 - 100.00**

□ Capitol EAP 1-2121, green label, 1964 .... **50.00 - 100.00**

❏   Capitol EAP 1-2121, cardboard picture sleeve,
    1964 (ILLUS.) .... **150.00 - 300.00**

4-BY THE BEATLES

(Contents: Honey Don't/I'm a Loser//Mr. Moonlight/
Everybody's Trying to Be My Baby)

❏ Capitol R-5365, orange and yellow swirl label, two type styles exist, 1965
(ILLUS.) .... **40.00 - 80.00**

❏ Capitol R-5365, cardboard picture sleeve, 1965
(ILLUS.) .... **100.00 - 200.00**

MEET THE BEATLES

(Contents: It Won't Be Long/This Boy/All My Loving//Don't
Bother Me/All I've Got to Do/I Wanna Be Your Man)

❏   Capitol SXA-2047, stereo jukebox edtion; small hole, plays at 33 1/3 rpm, 1964

(ILLUS.) .... **200.00 - 400.00**

❑ Capitol SXA-2047, picture sleeve, with five jukebox title strips and three miniature covers intact; deduct 33 percent if the strips and covers are missing, deduct less if material is there but not intact, 1964 (ILLUS.) .... **300.00 - 600.00**

OPEN-END INTERVIEW WITH THE BEATLES

(Contents: Interview/I Want to Hold Your Hand//This Boy/It
    Won't Be Long)

❏　Capitol PRO-2548/2549, promo only, black colorband label, small hole, plays at 33
　　1/3 rpm; counterfeit copies have an all-black label, 1964

　　(ILLUS.) .... **400.00 - 800.00**

❏ Capitol PRO-2548/2549, picture sleeve, contains script for interview on one side; authentic copies are glossy and have a die-cut thumb tab, 1964

(ILLUS.) ....**500.00 – 1,000.**

SOMETHING NEW

(Contents: I'll Cry Instead/And I Love Her/Slow Down//If I
     Fell/Tell Me Why/Matchbox)

❑   Capitol SXA-2108, stereo jukebox edtion; small hole, plays at 33 1/3 rpm, 1964
      (ILLUS.) .... **200.00 - 400.00**

Capitol SXA-2108, picture sleeve, with five jukebox title strips and three miniature covers intact; deduct 33 percent if the strips and covers are missing, deduct less if material is there but not intact, 1964 (ILLUS.) .... **300.00 - 600.00**

SOUVENIR OF THEIR VISIT TO AMERICA

(Contents: Misery/Taste of Honey//Ask Me Why/Anna)

❏ Vee Jay 1-903, black rainbow label, oval logo, all titles with same size print,
1964 .... **20.00 - 40.00**

❏ Vee Jay 1-903, black rainbow label, brackets logo, all titles with same size print,
three type styles exist, 1964 .... **45.00 - 90.00**

❏ Vee Jay 1-903, plain black label, oval logo, all titles with same size print,
1964 .... **62.50 - 125.00**

❏ Vee Jay 1-903, plain black label, brackets logo, all titles with same size print,
1964 .... **100.00 - 200.00**

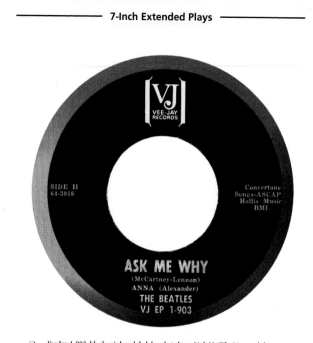

❑ Vee Jay 1-903, black rainbow label, brackets logo, "Ask Me Why" in much larger
print, two type styles exist, 1964

(ILLUS.) ....**62.50 - 125.00**

❑ Vee Jay 1-903, plain black label, "VEE JAY" stands alone, "Ask Me Why" in slightly

larger print, 1964 ....**75.00 - 150.00**

❏ Vee Jay 1-903, promo copy, white and blue label, all titles with same size print,

   1964 (ILLUS.) .... **200.00 - 400.00**

❏ Vee Jay 1-903, promo copy, white and blue label, "Ask Me Why" in much larger

   print, two type styles exist, 1964 .... **150.00 - 300.00**

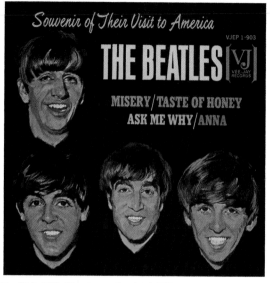

❏   Vee Jay 1-903, picture sleeve, cardboard stock, 1964
    (ILLUS.) .... **30.00 - 60.00**

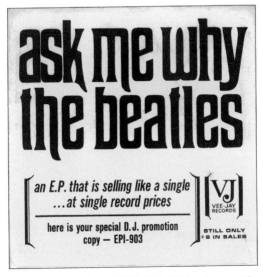

❏ Vee Jay 1-903, picture sleeve, "Ask Me Why/The Beatles" plugged on promo-only
sleeve, 1964 (ILLUS.) .... **6,000 – 8,000.**

12-Inch Singles

MERRY CHRISTMAS AND HAPPY NEW YEAR

❏ (no label) (no #), promo item from KYA Radio, San Francisco; B-side is blank,
1965 .... **250.00 - 500.00**

Albums

ABBEY ROAD

❑ Apple SO-383, with "Mfd. by Apple" on label; "Her Majesty" is NOT listed on the label, cover is fold-over "Shorepak" posterboard, 1969

(ILLUS.) .... **10.00 - 20.00**

- ❏ Apple SO-383, with "Mfd. by Apple" on label; "Her Majesty" may or may not be listed on label, but it is NOT listed on cover, which consists of slicks on cardboard, 1969 (ILLUS.) .... **10.00 - 20.00**
- ❏ Apple SO-383, with "Mfd. by Apple" on label; "Her Majesty" IS listed on the label, cover is fold-over "Shorepak" posterboard, 1969 .... **10.00 - 20.00**

❏ Apple SO-383, with Capitol logo on Side 2 bottom; "Her Majesty" is NOT listed on either the jacket or the label, 1969 .... **37.50 - 75.00**

❏ Apple SO-383, with Capitol logo on Side 2 bottom; "Her Majesty" IS listed on the label, some jackets list "Her Majesty" and some don't, 1969........... **20.00 - 40.00**

❏ Apple SO-383, with "All Rights Reserved" on label, either in black print or in light print along label edge (both versions exist), 1975......................... **12.50 - 25.00**

❏ Capitol SO-383, orange label, 1976 .... **6.00 - 12.00**

❏ Capitol SO-383, purple label, large Capitol logo, 1978 .... **5.00 - 10.00**

❏ Capitol SEAX-11900, picture disc; deduct 25% for cut-outs, 1978.... **20.00 - 40.00**

❏ Mobile Fidelity 1-023, "Original Master Recording" across top of front cover, 1979 .... **25.00 - 50.00**

❏ Capitol SO-383, black label, print in colorband, 1983 .... **7.50 - 15.00**

❏ Capitol SJ-383, new prefix; black label, print in colorband, 1984.... **15.00 - 30.00**

❏ Capitol C1-46446, new number; purple label, small Capitol logo, 1988.. **12.50 - 25.00**

❏ Capitol C1-46446, Apple logo restored to back cover on reissue, 1995.. **6.00 - 12.00**

AIN'T SHE SWEET

❏ Atco 33-169, mono, dark blue and gold label, "with Tony Sheridan" not on label or back cover, 1964 .... **200.00 - 400.00**

❏ Atco 33-169, mono, dark blue and gold label, "with Tony Sheridan" added to label and back cover, 1964 .... **100.00 - 200.00**

❏ Atco 33-169, mono, white label promo, 1964 ....**500.00 – 1,000.**

❏ Atco SD 33-169, stereo, tan and purple label, "with Tony Sheridan" not on label or back cover, 1964 .... **100.00 - 600.00**

❏ Atco SD 33-169, stereo, tan and purple label, "with Tony Sheridan" added to label and back cover, 1964 .... **200.00 - 400.00**

❏   Atco SD 33-169, stereo, yellow label, 1969................................**250.00 - 500.00**

ALL OUR LOVING

❏   Cicadelic 1963, 1986 ....**6.00 - 12.00**

THE AMAZING BEATLES AND OTHER GREAT ENGLISH GROUP SOUNDS

❏   Clarion 601, mono; among the 21 albums pictured on the back cover is the actual
front cover of this album, 1966 ....**50.00 - 100.00**

❏   Clarion 601, mono; among the 21 albums pictured on the back cover is the wrong
front cover design for this album, 1966 ....**60.00 - 120.00**

❏   Clarion SD 601, stereo, among the 21 albums pictured on the back cover is the
actual front cover of this album, 1966....................................**100.00 - 200.00**

❏   Clarion SD 601, stereo, among the 21 albums pictured on the back cover is the
wrong front cover design for this album, 1966........................**125.00 - 250.00**

THE AMERICAN TOUR WITH ED RUDY

❏   Radio Pulsebeat News 2, Yellow label; some copies came with a special edition of
Teen Talk magazine (add 50%),
1964..**50.00 - 100.00**

❏   Radio Pulsebeat News 2, Blue label; authorized reissue with Beatles' photo on
cover, 1980 ....**12.50 - 25.00**

ANTHOLOGY 1

❑ Apple C1-8-34445, three-record set, all copies distributed in the U.S. were manufactured in the U.K. with no distinguishing marks (some LPs imported directly from the U.K. have "Made in England" stickers, which can be removed easily), 1995 (ILLUS.) .... **20.00 - 40.00**

ANTHOLOGY 2

❑ Apple C1-8-34448, three-record set, made in U.S.A. version,
1996 (ILLUS.) ....**20.00 - 40.00**

ANTHOLOGY 2 SAMPLER

❑ Apple SPRO 11206/11207, eight-song promo-only collection sent to college radio
stations, 1996 (ILLUS.) ....**75.00 - 150.00**

ANTHOLOGY 3

❏ Apple C1-8-34451, three-record set, made in U.S.A. version,
1996 (ILLUS.) .... **15.00 - 30.00**

BEATLE TALK

❑ Great Northwest GNW 4007, 1978...**5.00 - 10.00**
❑ Great Northwest GNW 4007, Columbia Record Club edition; "CRC" on
   spine, 1978 ....**25.00 - 50.00**

BEATLEMANIA TOUR COVERAGE

❑ I-N-S Radio News DOC-1, promo-only open-end interview with script in plain white
   jacket, 1964 ....**1,000. – 1.500.**

THE BEATLES

(Also known as, but never actually titled, THE WHITE ALBUM.)

❏ Apple SWBO-101, two-record set, numbered copy with only "SWBO-101" at lower left of open gatefold; includes four individual photos and large poster (included in value); because the white cover shows ring wear so readily, this is an EXTREMELY difficult album to find in near-mint condition; first pressing label has Side 1, Song 5 incorrectly listed as "Bungalow Bill", 1968 (ILLUS.) .... **100.00 - 400.00**

This poster came with most copies of *The Beatles*. Unless
noted in the description, this poster must be with the
album for it to be considered complete.

❑ Apple SWBO-101, two-record set, numbered copy with only "SWBO-101" at lower
left of open gatefold; includes four individual photos and large poster (included in
value); because the white cover shows ring wear so readily, this is an EXTREMELY
difficult album to find in near-mint condition; second pressing label has Side 1,
Song 5 correctly listed as "The Continuing Story of Bungalow Bill",
1968..**75.00 - 200.00**

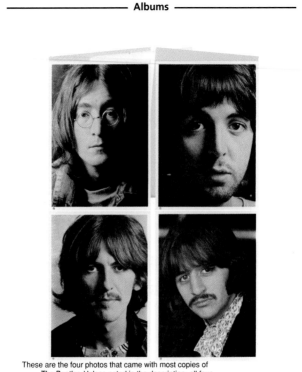

These are the four photos that came with most copies of
The Beatles. Unless noted in the description, all four
of these photos must be with the album for it to be
complete.

❏ Apple SWBO-101, two-record set, numbered copy with "SWBO-101" and "© Apple Records, Inc." at lower left of open gatefold; includes four individual photos and large poster (included in value); because the white cover shows ring wear so readily, this is an EXTREMELY difficult album to find in near-mint condition,

1968...**40.00 - 100.00**

❏ Apple SWBO-101, two-record set, un-numbered copy; embossed title on front cover; includes four individual photos and large poster (included in value),

1970...**30.00 - 60.00**

❏ Apple SWBO-101, two-record set, with "All Rights Reserved" on labels; title in black on cover; photos and poster of thinner stock than originals,

1975...**37.50 - 70.00**

❏ Capitol SWBO-101, two-record set, orange label; with photos and poster,

1976...**15.00 - 30.00**

❏ Capitol SWBO-101, two-record set, purple label, large Capitol logo; with photos and poster (some copies have four photos as one perforated sheet),

1978...**15.00 - 30.00**

❏ Capitol SEBX-11841, two-record set, white vinyl; with photos and poster (with number "SEBX-11841" on each), 1978.........................**25.00 - 50.00**

❏ Mobile Fidelity 2-072, two-record set, "Original Master Recording" on front cover; not issued with photos or poster, 1982...................................**25.00 - 50.00**

❏ Capitol SWBO-101, two-record set, black label, print in colorband; with photos and poster (some copies have four photos as one perforated sheet),

1983...**20.00 - 40.00**

❏ Capitol C1-46443, two-record set, new number; purple label, small Capitol logo; with photos and poster (some copies have four photos as one perforated sheet),

1988...**25.00 - 50.00**

❏ Capitol C1-46443, two-record set, with Apple logo on back cover,

1995...**10.00 - 20.00**

THE BEATLES AGAIN

See HEY JUDE.

THE BEATLES AND FRANK IFIELD ON STAGE

Also see JOLLY WHAT! THE BEATLES AND FRANK IFIELD ON STAGE.

❏ Vee Jay LP 1085, mono ("VJ 1085" at lower right cover), portrait of Beatles on cover; authentic copies are dark blue; counterfeits are bright blue and have no spine print, 1964...**3,000. – 5,000.**

❏ Vee Jay SR 1085, stereo ("STEREO" at center top cover), portrait of Beatles on cover; authentic copies are dark blue; counterfeits are bright blue and have neither spine print nor the word "STEREO" at the top, 1964................**8,000. – 12,000.**

❑ Vee Jay SR 1085, any counterfeit version......................................**10.00 - 20.00**

THE BEATLES AT THE HOLLYWOOD BOWL

❑ Capitol SMAS-11638, custom tan label, with embossed title and tickets on front
cover, 1977 ....**10.00 - 20.00**

❑ Capitol SMAS-11638, promo, tan label in plain white jacket with "Advance
Pressing: The Beatles at the Hollywood Bowl" stamped on it,
1977 ....**250.00 - 500.00**

❑ Capitol SMAS-11638, without embossed title and tickets, 1980 .... **7.50 - 15.00**

❑ Capitol SMAS-11638, with UPC code on back cover, 1989 ....**20.00 - 40.00**

THE BEATLES — CIRCA 1960 — IN THE BEGINNING
FEATURING TONY SHERIDAN

❑ Polydor 24-4504, stereo, gatefold cover, red label with full title,
1970 ....**12.50 - 25.00**

❑ Polydor 24-4504, stereo, gatefold cover, red label with only the title "The Beatles
-- In the Beginning", 1970s ....**20.00 - 40.00**

❑ Polydor SKAO-93199, stereo, Capitol Record Club edition, 1970 .....**20.00 - 40.00**

❑ Polydor PD-4504, stereo, reissue without gatefold cover, 1981..........**6.00 - 12.00**

❑ Polydor 825 073-1, stereo, reissue with new number, 1988..............**10.00 - 20.00**

THE BEATLES COLLECTION

❑ Capitol BC-13, 15-record box set, contains each of the original 13 British LPs in
separate jackets plus the British version of Rarities; individually numbered series
of approximately 3,300 copies; American versions have "EMI" and "BC-13" on box
spine, whereas imported versions tend to have "Parlophone" on the spine; imports
are much more common than the U.S. edition, 1978................**125.00 - 250.00**

❑ Mobile Fidelity BC-1, 14-record box set, contains each of the original 13 British
LPs in separate jackets; numbered edition of 25,000; includes Geo-Disc cartridge
alignment tool, 1982 ....**250.00 - 500.00**

THE BEATLES COLLECTION PLATINUM SERIES

❏   Capitol (no #), 18-record box set, promotional item issued to help introduce
    Capitol's short-lived line of computer software, 1984 .... **400.00 - 800.00**

THE BEATLES DELUXE BOX SET

❏   Capitol BBX1-91302, 16-record box set; contains each of the original 13 British LPs
    in separate jackets plus Past Masters Volumes 1 and 2; comes in roll-top oak box
    with information booklet, 1988 .... **150.00 - 300.00**

BEATLES FOR SALE

❏   Mobile Fidelity 1-104, stereo, "Original Master Recording" on top of front cover;
    first U.S. edition of album originally released in Britain in 1964,
    1986 .... **20.00 - 40.00**
❏   Capitol CLJ-46438, mono, black label, print in colorband; first Capitol version of
    original British LP, 1987 .... **10.00 - 20.00**
❏   Capitol CLJ-46438, mono, purple label, small Capitol logo at top,
    1988 .... **12.50 - 25.00**
❏   Capitol C1-46438, mono, new prefix; Apple logo on back cover,
    1995 .... **6.00 - 12.00**

THE BEATLES 1962-1966

❏ Apple SKBO-3403, two-record set, custom red Apple labels, comes with two red lyric innersleeves and a single-page discography insert, 1973

(ILLUS.) .... **15.00 - 30.00**

❑ Apple SKBO-3403, two-record set, custom red Apple labels with "All Rights
   Reserved" on labels, 1975 .... **25.00 - 50.00**
❑ Capitol SKBO-3403, two-record set, red labels, 1976 .... **10.00 - 20.00**
❑ Capitol SKBO-3403, two-record set, blue labels (error pressing),
   1976 .... **15.00 - 30.00**
❑ Capitol SEBX-11842, two-record set, red vinyl, 1978 .... **20.00 - 40.00**
❑ Capitol C1-90435, two-record set, new number; purple labels, small Capitol logo,
   1988 .... **15.00 - 30.00**
❑ Apple C1-97036, two-record set, custom red Apple labels; red vinyl; all copies
   pressed in U.K; U.S. versions have a bar-code sticker over the international bar
   code on back cover, 1993 .... **12.50 - 25.00**

THE BEATLES 1967-1970

❏   Apple SKBO-3404, two-record set, custom blue Apple labels, comes with two blue
    lyric innersleeves and a single-page discography insert, 1973
    (ILLUS.) .... **15.00 - 30.00**
❏   Apple SKBO-3404, two-record set, custom blue Apple labels with "All Rights
    Reserved" on labels, 1975... **25.00 - 50.00**
❏   Capitol SKBO-3404, two-record set, blue labels, 1976.................... **10.00 - 20.00**
❏   Capitol SEBX-11843, two-record set, blue vinyl, 1978.................... **20.00 - 40.00**
❏   Capitol C1-90438, two-record set, new number; purple labels, small Capitol logo,
    1988.. **15.00 - 30.00**
❏   Apple C1-97039, Custom blue Apple labels; blue vinyl; all copies pressed in U.K.;
    U.S. versions have a bar-code sticker over the international bar code on back cover,
    1993.. **12.50 - 25.00**

BEATLES VI

❏ Capitol T 2358, mono, black labe with colorband, with "See label for correct
playing order" on back cover, 1965 (ILLUS.)..............................**60.00 - 120.00**

❏ Capitol T 2358, mono, black label with colorband, with song titles listed in correct order on back cover, 1965 (ILLUS.) .... **50.00 - 100.00**

❏ Capitol ST 2358, stereo, black label with colorband; with "See label for correct playing order" on back cover, 1965 .... **50.00 - 100.00**

❏   Capitol ST 2358, stereo, black label with colorband; with song titles listed in correct

order on back cover, 1965 (ILLUS.) .... **40.00 - 80.00**

❏ Capitol ST 2358, stereo, black colorband label; border print adds "A Subsidiary of
Capitol Industries Inc.," 1968..**25.00 - 50.00**

❏ Capitol ST 2358, stereo, lime green label, 1969..............................**20.00 - 40.00**

❏ Capitol ST-8-2358, stereo, Capitol Record Club edition; black label with colorband,
1969...**250.00 - 500.00**

❏ Capitol ST-8-2358, stereo, Capitol Record Club edition; lime green label,
1969...**200.00 - 400.00**

❏ Apple/Capitol ST 2358, stereo, Apple label with Capitol logo on Side 2 bottom, cover
still says "Capitol," 1971 ....**20.00 - 40.00**

❏ Apple/Capitol ST 2358, stereo, with "Mfd. by Apple" on label, cover still says
"Capitol," 1971..**10.00 - 20.00**

❏ Apple/Capitol ST 2358, stereo, Apple label with "All Rights Reserved" on label, cover
still says "Capitol," 1975 ....**12.50 - 25.00**

❏ Capitol ST 2358, stereo, orange label, 1976................................**6.00 - 12.00**

❏ Capitol ST 2358, stereo, purple label, large Capitol logo at top,
1978..**5.00 - 10.00**

❏ Capitol ST 2358, mono, black label, print in colorband; though the cover and label
say "Stereo," the record plays in mono, 1983...................................**7.50 - 15.00**

❏ Capitol ST 2358, mono. purple label, small Capitol logo at top; though the cover
and label say "Stereo," the record plays in mono, 1988.................**40.00 - 80.00**

❏ Capitol C1-90445, mono, new number; purple label, small Capitol logo at top;
though the cover and label say "Stereo," the record plays in mono,
1988..**12.50 - 25.00**

BEATLES '65

- ❏ Capitol T 2228, mono, black label with colorband,
  1964 (ILLUS.) .... 60.00 - 120.00
- ❏ Capitol ST 2228, stereo, black label with colorband,
  1964 .... 40.00 - 80.00

- ❏ Capitol ST 2228, stereo, black colorband label; border print adds "A Subsidiary of Capitol Industries Inc."; most covers also add "GOLD RECORD AWARD" seal to front cover, 1968 .... **25.00 - 50.00**
- ❏ Capitol ST 2228, stereo, lime green label, 1969 .... **20.00 - 40.00**
- ❏ Apple/Capitol ST 2228, stereo, Apple label with Capitol logo on Side 2 bottom, cover still says "Capitol," 1971 .... **20.00 - 40.00**
- ❏ Apple/Capitol ST 2228, stereo, with "Mfd. by Apple" on label, cover still says "Capitol," 1971 .... **10.00 - 20.00**
- ❏ Apple/Capitol ST 2228, stereo, Apple label with "All Rights Reserved" on label, cover still says "Capitol," 1975 .... **12.50 - 25.00**
- ❏ Capitol ST 2228, stereo, orange label, 1976 .... **6.00 - 12.00**
- ❏ Capitol ST 2228, stereo, purple label, large Capitol logo at top, 1978 .... **5.00 - 10.00**
- ❏ Capitol ST 2228, stereo, black label, print in colorband, 1983 .... **7.50 - 15.00**
- ❏ Capitol C1-90446, stereo, new number; purple label, small Capitol logo at top, 1988 .... **12.50 - 25.00**

THE BEATLES SPECIAL LIMITED EDITION

- ❏ Apple/Capitol (no #), 10-record box set; contains Apple-label editions of Meet the Beatles!, Something New, Beatles '65, The Early Beatles, Rubber Soul, Revolver, Sgt. Pepper's Lonely Hearts Club Band, Magical Mystery Tour, Abbey Road and Hey Jude, 1974 .... **600.00 – 1,200.**

THE BEATLES TALK WITH JERRY G.

- ❏ Backstage BSR-1165, picture disc, 1982 .... **12.50 - 25.00**

THE BEATLES TALK WITH JERRY G., VOL. 2

- ❏ Backstage BSR-1175, picture disc, 1983 .... **12.50 - 25.00**

THE BEATLES 10TH ANNIVERSARY BOX SET

❑ Apple/Capitol (no #), 19-record box set , promo only, used as an in-house premium at Capitol for executives and sales representatives; contains sealed Apple-label editions of 17 albums: Meet the Beatles!, The Beatles' Second Album, Something New, The Beatles' Story, Beatles '65, The Early Beatles, Beatles VI, Help!, Rubber Soul, Yesterday and Today, Revolver, Sgt. Pepper's Lonely Hearts Club Band, Magical Mystery Tour, The Beatles, Yellow Submarine, Abbey Road and Hey Jude (it did not include Let It Be), 1974 .... **1,500. – 2,000.**

THE BEATLES VS. THE FOUR SEASONS

❑ Vee Jay DX-30, two-record set, mono, contains records of Introducing the Beatles (1062) and Golden Hits of the Four Seasons (1065), 1964 .... **400.00 - 800.00**

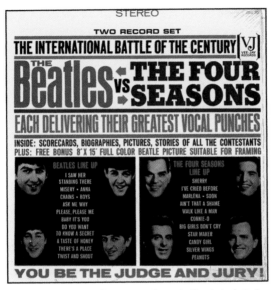

❑ Vee Jay DXS-30, two-record set, stereo, contains records of Introducing the Beatles (1062) and Golden Hits of the Four Seasons (1065), 1964

(ILLUS.) .... **2,500. – 4,000.**

❏ Vee Jay DX(S)-30, poster that came with previous, 1964,
add... (ILLUS.) .... **150.00 - 300.00**

THE BEATLES WITH TONY SHERIDAN AND THEIR GUESTS

(NOTE: The title as listed on the front cover is THE BEATLES WITH TONY SHERIDAN AND GUESTS.)

❏ MGM E-4215, mono, with "And Others" under the list of song titles on the front
cover, 1964 .... **125.00 - 250.00**

❏ MGM E-4215, mono, without "And Others" under the list of song titles on the front
cover, 1964 .... **100.00 - 200.00**

❏ MGM SE-4215, stereo, with "And Others" under the list of song titles on the front
cover, 1964 .... **300.00 - 600.00**

❏ MGM SE-4215, stereo, without "And Others" under the list of song titles on the
front cover, 1964 .... **400.00 - 800.00**

THE BEATLES' CHRISTMAS ALBUM

❏ Apple SBC-100, mono, fan club issue of the seven Christmas messages; authentic
copies have crisp and clear labels, whereas many counterfeits have blurry labels;
authentic copies are composed of slicks pasted on cardboard, whereas many
counterfeits are composed of one-piece wrap-around covers; authentic copies have
a medium blue color, and many counterfeits are a lighter blue; all authentic copies
are black vinyl, thus all colored vinyl copier are counterfeits, 1970
(ILLUS.) .... **200.00 - 400.00**

THE BEATLES' FIRST LIVE RECORDINGS, VOLUME 1

❏   Pickwick SPC-3661, mono, recorded live in Hamburg, 1979............ **6.00 - 12.00**

THE BEATLES' FIRST LIVE RECORDINGS, VOLUME 2

❏   Pickwick SPC-3662, mono, recorded live in Hamburg, 1979............ **6.00 - 12.00**

THE BEATLES' SECOND ALBUM

❑ Capitol T 2080, mono, black label with colorband, first label has no times listed next to "Long Tall Sally" or "I Call Your Name," 1964
(ILLUS.) .... **100.00 - 200.00**
❑ Capitol T 2080, mono, black label with colorband, second label has times listed next to "Long Tall Sally" and "I Call Your Name," 1964 .... **75.00 - 150.00**

❏   Capitol ST 2080, stereo, black label with colorband, first label has no times listed
     next to "Long Tall Sally" or "I Call Your Name," and "ASCAP" is next to "I Call
     Your Name," 1964 (ILLUS.)..**60.00 - 120.00**
❏   Capitol ST 2080, stereo, black label with colorband, second label has times listed
     next to "Long Tall Sally" and "I Call Your Name," 1964..............**50.00 - 100.00**

❏ Capitol ST 2080, stereo, black label with colorband, third label has time listed next to "Long Tall Sally," and "I Call Your Name" has "BMI" and no time after it, 1966? (ILLUS.)..**40.00 - 80.00**

❑ Capitol ST 2080, stereo, black label with colorband, fourth label has no times listed next to "Long Tall Sally" or "I Call Your Name," and "BMI" is next to "I Call Your Name," 1967? .... **40.00 - 80.00**

❑ Capitol ST 2080, stereo, black colorband label; border print adds "A Subsidiary of Capitol Industries Inc."; most of these add "GOLD RECORD AWARD" seal to front cover, 1968 .... **25.00 - 50.00**

❑ Capitol ST 2080, stereo, lime green label, 1969 .... **20.00 - 40.00**

❑ Capitol ST-8-2080, stereo, Capitol Record Club edition; black label with colorband, 1969 .... **250.00 - 500.00**

❑ Capitol ST-8-2080, stereo, Capitol Record Club edition; lime green label, 1969 .... **150.00 - 300.00**

❑ Apple/Capitol ST 2080, stereo, Apple label with Capitol logo on Side 2 bottom, cover still says "Capitol," 1971 .... **20.00 - 40.00**

❑ Apple/Capitol ST 2080, stereo. with "Mfd. by Apple" on label, cover still says "Capitol," 1971 .... **10.00 - 20.00**

❑ Apple/Capitol ST 2080, stereo, Apple label with "All Rights Reserved" on label, cover still says "Capitol," 1975 .... **12.50 - 25.00**

❑ Capitol ST 2080, stereo, orange label, 1976 .... **6.00 - 12.00**

❑ Capitol ST 2080, stereo, purple label, large Capitol logo at top, 1978 .... **5.00 - 10.00**

❑ Capitol ST 2080, stereo, black label, print in colorband, 1983 .... **7.50 - 15.00**

❑ Capitol C1-90444, stereo, new number; purple label, small Capitol logo at top, 1988 .... **12.50 - 25.00**

THE BEATLES' STORY

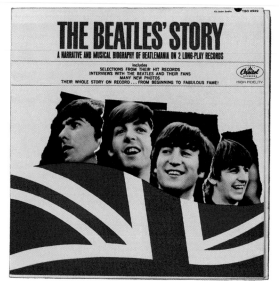

❏ Capitol TBO 2222, 2-record set, mono, black label with colorband, records have
Side 1 backed with Side 4 and Side 2 backed with Side 3,
1964 (ILLUS.) .... **100.00 - 200.00**
❏ Capitol TBO 2222, 2-record set, mono, black label with colorband, records have Side
1 backed with Side 2 and Side 3 backed with Side 4, 1964 .... **150.00 - 300.00**

❏ Capitol STBO 2222, 2-record set, stereo, black label with colorband, all known sets have Side 1 backed with Side 4 and Side 2 backed with Side 3, 1964 .... **150.00 - 300.00**

❏ Capitol STBO 2222, 2-record set, stereo, black colorband label; border print adds "A Subsidiary of Capitol Industries Inc.," 1968 .... **40.00 - 80.00**

❏ Capitol STBO 2222, 2-record set, stereo, lime green label, 1969 .... **25.00 - 50.00**

❏ Apple/Capitol STBO 2222, 2-record set, stereo, Apple labels with Capitol logo on bottom of B-side of both records, cover still says "Capitol," 1971 .... **25.00 - 50.00**

❏ Apple/Capitol STBO 2222, 2-record set, stereo, with "Mfd. by Apple" on labels, cover still says "Capitol," 1971 .... **15.00 - 30.00**

❏ Apple/Capitol STBO 2222, 2-record set, stereo, Apple labels with "All Rights Reserved" on labels, cover still says "Capitol," 1975 .... **20.00 - 40.00**

❏ Capitol STBO 2222, 2-record set, stereo, orange labels, 1976 .... **10.00 - 20.00**

❏ Capitol STBO 2222, 2-record set, stereo, purple labels, large Capitol logo at top, 1978 .... **10.00 - 20.00**

❏ Capitol STBO 2222, 2-record set, stereo, black label, print in colorband, 1983 .... **20.00 - 40.00**

THE BRITISH ARE COMING

❏ Silhouette SM-10013, interview album with numbered sticker (very low numbers increase the value), black vinyl, 1984 .... **7.50 - 15.00**

❏ Silhouette SM-10013, interview album with numbered sticker (very low numbers increase the value), red vinyl, 1984 .... **40.00 - 80.00**

❏ Silhouette SM-10013, white label promo; no numbered sticker, 1984 .... **20.00 - 40.00**

❏ Silhouette PD-83010, picture disc, 1985 .... **15.00 - 30.00**

THE COMPLETE SILVER BEATLES

❏ Audio Rarities AR-2452, mono, contains 12 Decca audition tracks,
1982 .... **7.50 - 15.00**

THE DAVID WIGG INTERVIEWS (THE BEATLES TAPES)

❏ PBR International 7005/6, two-record set, blue vinyl, 1978 .... **40.00 - 80.00**
❏ PBR International 7005/6, two-record set, black vinyl, 1980 .... **30.00 - 60.00**

DAWN OF THE SILVER BEATLES

❏ United Distributors UDL-2333, mono, hand-stamped numbers on back cover and
label; contains 10 Decca audition tracks, 1981 .... **30.00 - 60.00**
❏ United Distributors UDL-2333, mono, with numbered registration card (deduct
20% if missing), 1981 .... **25.00 - 50.00**

THE EARLY BEATLES

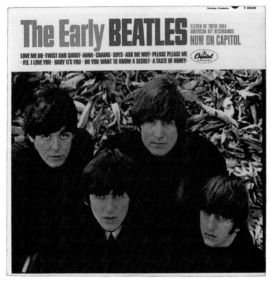

- ❏ Capitol T 2309, mono, black label with colorband, 1965 (ILLUS.) .... **100.00 - 200.00**
- ❏ Capitol ST 2309, stereo, black label with colorband, 1965 .... **50.00 - 100.00**

❏ Capitol ST 2309, stereo, black colorband label; border print adds "A Subsidiary of Capitol Industries Inc.", 1968...**25.00 - 50.00**

❏ Capitol ST 2309, stereo, lime green label, 1969.............................**20.00 - 40.00**

❏ Apple/Capitol ST 2309, stereo, Apple label with Capitol logo on Side 2 bottom, cover still says "Capitol," 1971...**20.00 - 40.00**

❏ Apple/Capitol ST 2309, stereo, with "Mfd. by Apple" on label, cover still says "Capitol," 1971...**10.00 - 20.00**

❏ Apple/Capitol ST 2309, stereo, Apple label with "All Rights Reserved" on label, cover still says "Capitol," 1975...**12.50 - 25.00**

❏ Capitol ST 2309, stereo, orange label, 1976.......................................**6.00 - 12.00**

❏ Capitol ST 2309, stereo, purple label, large Capitol logo at top, 1978...**5.00 - 10.00**

❏ Capitol ST 2309, stereo, black label, print in colorband, 1983 ....**12.50 - 25.00**

EAST COAST INVASION

❏ Cicadelic 1964, 1985...**6.00 - 12.00**

FIRST MOVEMENT

❏ Audiofidelity PHX-339, mono, contains eight Decca audition tracks; black vinyl 1982...**6.00 - 12.00**

❏ Audiofidelity PD-339, mono, contains eight Decca audition tracks; picture disc, 1982...**15.00 - 30.00**

FROM BRITAIN WITH BEAT!

❏ Cicadelic 1967, 1987...**6.00 - 12.00**

GOLDEN BEATLES

❏ Silhouette SM-10015, black vinyl, 1985 ....**7.50 - 15.00**

❏ Silhouette SM-10015, gold vinyl, 1985..**40.00 - 80.00**

THE GREAT AMERICAN TOUR — 1965 LIVE BEATLEMANIA CONCERT

❑ Lloyds ER-MC-LTD, Another interview album from the Ed Rudy people, with a live Beatles show in the background and the songs poorly overdubbed by the Liverpool Lads, 1965 ....**300.00 - 600.00**

A HARD DAY'S NIGHT

Also see UNITED ARTISTS PRESENTS A HARD DAY'S NIGHT.

❑ United Artists UAL 3366, mono, with "I Cry Instead" on label, publishing on back cover credited to "Unart" and "Maclen" for all songs except "This Boy," 1964 .... **100.00 - 200.00**

❑ United Artists UAL 3366, mono, with "I Cry Instead" on label, publishing on back cover credited to "Unart" and "Maclen" for all songs except "I'll Cry Instead" and "This Boy," 1964 .... **100.00 - 200.00**

❑ United Artists UAL 3366, mono, with "I'll Cry Instead" on label, 1964 .... **125.00 - 250.00**

❑ United Artists UAL 3366, mono, white label promo, 1964 .... **1,500. – 3,000.**

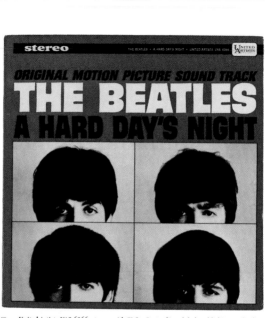

❏   United Artists UAS 6366, stereo, with "I Cry Instead" on label, publishing on back cover credited to "Unart" and "Maclen" for all songs except "This Boy,"

     1964 (ILLUS.) .... **100.00 - 200.00**

❏   United Artists UAS 6366, stereo, with "I Cry Instead" on label, publishing on back cover credited to "Unart" and "Maclen" for all songs except "I'll Cry Instead" and

     "This Boy," 1964 .... **100.00 - 200.00**

❑ United Artists UAS 6366, stereo, with "I'll Cry Instead" on label.,
1964 .... **125.00 - 250.00**

❑ United Artists UAS 6366, stereo, pink vinyl; only one copy known, probably privately
and secretly done by a pressing-plant employee, 1964 .... **9,000. – 12,000.**

❑ United Artists T-90828. mono, Capitol Record Club edition,
1966 .... **1,000. – 1,500.**

❑ United Artists ST-90828, stereo, Capitol Record Club edition,
1966 (ILLUS.) .... **375.00 - 750.00**

- ❏ United Artists UAS 6366, stereo, pink and orange label, 1968.......... **25.00 - 50.00**
- ❏ United Artists UAS 6366, stereo, black and orange label, 1970 .... **25.00 - 50.00**
- ❏ United Artists UAS 6366, stereo, tan label, 1971............................. **10.00 - 20.00**
- ❏ United Artists UAS 6366, stereo, tan label with "All Rights Reserved" in perimeter print, 1975.. **10.00 - 20.00**
- ❏ United Artists UAS 6366, stereo, sunrise label; any of the variations from 1968 on can have titles of songs incorrectly listed as "I Cry Instead" and "Tell Me Who," or only one can be wrong, or neither can be wrong; there is no difference in value at this time, 1977.. **10.00 - 20.00**
- ❏ Capitol SW-11921, stereo, purple label, large Capitol logo, 1979...... **6.00 - 12.00**
- ❏ Capitol SW-11921, stereo, black label, print in colorband, 1983 .... **7.50 - 15.00**
- ❏ Mobile Fidelity 1-103, stereo, "Original Master Recording" at top of front cover; British version of album, 1987 .... **20.00 - 40.00**
- ❏ Capitol CLJ-46437, mono, black label, print in colorband; first Capitol version of original British LP, 1987.. **10.00 - 20.00**
- ❏ Capitol CLJ-46437, mono, British version of LP; purple label, small Capitol logo, 1988... **12.50 - 25.00**
- ❏ Capitol SW-11921, stereo, purple label, small Capitol logo, 1988.... **12.50 - 25.00**
- ❏ Capitol C1-46437, mono, new prefix; Apple logo on back cover, 1995... **6.00 - 12.00**

HEAR THE BEATLES TELL ALL

- ❏ Vee Jay PRO 202. white label promo with blue print, 1964..**12,000. – 18,000.**

❑ Vee Jay PRO 202, mono, with "VJLP 202" on label,
1964 (ILLUS.) .... **150.00 - 300.00**

❏ Vee Jay PRO 202, mono, with "VJLP 202 PRO" on label and "Interviews by Jim Steck
    and Dave Hull" above center hole, 1964 (ILLUS.) .... **100.00 - 200.00**
❏ Vee Jay PRO 202, "STEREO" on cover, with "VJLP 202 PRO" on label and
    "Interviews by Jim Steck and Dave Hull" below center hole
    1979 .... **5.00 - 10.00**

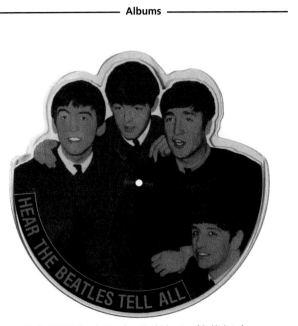

❏ Vee Jay PRO 202, shaped picture disc with edited version of the black vinyl
recordings, 1987 (ILLUS.) .... **10.00 - 20.00**

HELP!

Also see UNITED ARTISTS PRESENTS HELP!

❑ Capitol MAS 2386, mono, black label with colorband; first edition labels do not mention Ken Thorne as composer of "In the Tyrol," "The Bitter End" and "The Chase," 1965 (ILLUS.) ....100.00 - 200.00

❑ Capitol MAS 2386, mono, black label with colorband; later edition labels add Ken Thorne as composer of "In the Tyrol," "The Bitter End" and "The Chase" and add "You Can't Do That" to the Side 2 contents under "The Bitter End," 1965 ....75.00 - 150.00

☐   Capitol SMAS 2386, stereo, black label with colorband, first edition labels do not mention Ken Thorne as composer of "In the Tyrol," "The Bitter End" and "The Chase," 1965 (ILLUS.) ....**75.00 - 150.00**

❏ Capitol SMAS 2386, stereo, black label with colorband, second edition labels add Ken Thorne as composer of "In the Tyrol," "The Bitter End" and "The Chase," 1965 (ILLUS.) ....**50.00 - 100.00**

❏ Capitol SMAS 2386, stereo, black label with colorband, later edition labels add Ken Thorne as composer of "In the Tyrol," "The Bitter End" and "The Chase" and add "You Can't Do That" to the Side 2 contents under "The Bitter End," 1965 .... **40.00 - 80.00**

❏ Capitol SMAS 2386, stereo, black colorband label; border print adds "A Subsidiary of Capitol Industries Inc.", 1968 .... **25.00 - 50.00**

❏ Capitol SMAS 2386, stereo, lime green label, 1969 .... **20.00 - 40.00**

❏ Capitol SMAS-8-2386, stereo, Capitol Record Club edition; black label with colorband; no "8" on spine, 1969 .... **200.00 - 400.00**

❏ Capitol SMAS-8-2386, stereo, Capitol Record Club edition; black label with colorband; with "8" on spine, 1969 .... **300.00 - 600.00**

❏ Capitol SMAS-8-2386, stereo, Capitol Record Club edition; lime green label; no "8" on spine, 1969 .... **100.00 - 200.00**

❏ Capitol SMAS-8-2386, stereo, Capitol Record Club edition; lime green label; with "8" on spine, 1969 .... **200.00 - 400.00**

❏ Capitol SMAS-8-2386, stereo, Longines Symphonette edition; with "Mfd. by Longines" and "8" on cover, 1971 .... **350.00 - 700.00**

❏ Apple/Capitol SMAS 2386, stereo, Apple label with Capitol logo on Side 2 bottom, cover still says "Capitol," 1971 .... **20.00 - 40.00**

❏ Apple/Capitol SMAS 2386, stereo, with "Mfd. by Apple" on label, cover still says "Capitol," 1971 .... **10.00 - 20.00**

❏ Apple/Capitol SMAS 2386, stereo, Apple label with "All Rights Reserved" on label, cover still says "Capitol," 1975 .... **12.50 - 25.00**

❏ Capitol SMAS 2386, stereo, orange label, 1976 .... **6.00 - 12.00**

❏ Capitol SMAS 2386, stereo, purple label, large Capitol logo at top, 1978 .... **5.00 - 10.00**

❏ Capitol SMAS 2386, stereo, black label, print in colorband, 1983 ...... **7.50 - 15.00**

❏ Mobile Fidelity 1-105, stereo, "Original Master Recording" at top of front cover, British version of album, 1985 .... **20.00 - 40.00**

❏ Capitol CLJ-46439, stereo, first Capitol version of original British LP; black label,
print in colorband, 1987 .... **10.00 - 20.00**
❏ Capitol CLJ-46439, stereo, British version of album; purple label, small Capitol logo
at top, 1988 .... **12.50 - 25.00**
❏ Capitol C1-90454, stereo, new number for American version; purple label, small
Capitol logo at top, 1988 .... **12.50 - 25.00**
❏ Capitol C1-46439, stereo, British version of album; new prefix; Apple logo on back
cover, 1995 .... **6.00 - 12.00**

HERE, THERE AND EVERYWHERE

❏ Cicadelic 1968, 1988 .... **6.00 - 12.00**

HEY JUDE

❑ Apple SO-385, prototype covers with "Beatles Again" on cover above a potted plant;
one version has this on the front, the other on the back; these are covers ONLY and
have nothing to do with anything on the record labels,

1970 (ILLUS.) .... **6,000 – 8,000.**

- ❏ Apple SW-385, label calls the LP "The Beatles Again"; record number on label is "SO-385", 1970 (ILLUS.) .... **20.00 - 40.00**
- ❏ Apple SW-385, label calls the LP "The Beatles Again"; record number on label is "SW-385", 1970 .... **12.50 - 25.00**
- ❏ Apple SW-385, with Capitol logo on Side 2 bottom; label calls the LP "Hey Jude", 1970 .... **37.50 - 75.00**

❏   Apple SW-385, with "Mfd. by Apple" on label; label calls the LP "Hey Jude",
    1970 (ILLUS.) .... **10.00 - 20.00**

❏ Apple SW-385, with "All Rights Reserved" on label; label calls the LP "Hey Jude",
1975..**12.50 - 25.00**
❏ Capitol SW-385, orange label (all Capitol label versions call the LP "Hey Jude"),
1976..**6.00 - 12.00**
❏ Capitol SW-385, purple label, large Capitol logo, 1978...................**5.00 - 10.00**
❏ Capitol SW-385, black label, print in colorband,
1983..**25.00 - 50.00**
❏ Capitol SJ-385, new prefix; black label, print in colorband,
1984..**15.00 - 30.00**
❏ Capitol C1-90442, new number; purple label, small Capitol logo,
1988..**12.50 - 25.00**

THE HISTORIC FIRST LIVE RECORDINGS

❏ Pickwick PTP-2098, two-record set, same contents as Lingasong LP, plus the non-
Beatles track "Hully Gully", 1980...**9.00 - 18.00**

I APOLOGIZE

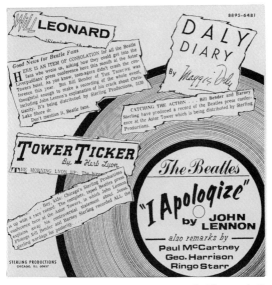

- ❑ Sterling 8895-6481, one-sided LP with John Lennon's "apology" for supposed anti-Christian remarks; includes photo, 1966 (ILLUS.) .... **200.00 - 400.00**
- ❑ Sterling 8895-6481, same as above, but without photo, 1966 .... **150.00 - 300.00**

INTRODUCING THE BEATLES

❑ Vee Jay LP 1062, mono ("LP 1062" in lower right corner of front cover); "ad back" (25 "other fine albums of significant interest" pictured on back cover); with "Love Me Do" and "P.S. I Love You"; black label with coloband, oval Vee Jay logo, 1964 (ILLUS.) .... **2,500. – 4,000.**

❑ Vee Jay LP 1062, mono ("LP 1062" in lower right corner of front cover); blank back cover; with "Love Me Do" and "P.S. I Love You"; black label with coloband, oval Vee Jay logo, 1964 ....**800.00 – 1,200.**

INTRODUCING THE BEATLES

side one

I SAW HER
STANDING THERE

MISERY

ANNA

CHAINS

BOYS

LOVE ME DO

side two

P.S. I LOVE YOU

BABY IT'S YOU

DO YOU WANT
TO KNOW A SECRET?

A TASTE OF HONEY

THERE'S A PLACE

TWIST AND SHOUT

AMERICA'S GREATEST RECORDING ARTISTS ARE ON VEE-JAY RECORDS

❑ Vee Jay LP 1062, mono ("LP 1062" in lower right corner of front cover); song titles
cover; with "Love Me Do" and "P.S. I Love You"; black label with coloband, oval Vee
Jay logo, 1964 (ILLUS.) .... **400.00 - 800.00**

❑ Vee Jay LP 1062, mono ("LP 1062" in lower right corner of front cover); song titles
cover; with "Love Me Do" and "P.S. I Love You"; black label with coloband, oval Vee
Jay logo, 45-rpm-sized label with "Vee Jay" much closer to the rainbow ring than
on regular Vee-Jay labels, 1964 .... **500.00 – 1,000.**

❑ Vee Jay LP 1062, mono ("LP 1062" in lower right corner of front cover); song titles
cover; with "Love Me Do" and "P.S. I Love You"; black label with coloband, brackets
Vee Jay logo, 1964 .... **2,000. – 3,000.**

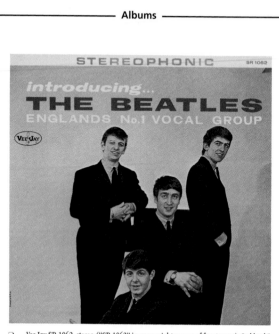

- Vee Jay SR 1062, stereo ("SR 1062" in upper right corner of front cover); "ad back" (25 "other fine albums of significant interest" pictured on back cover); with "Love Me Do" and "P.S. I Love You"; black label with coloband, oval Vee Jay logo, 1964 (ILLUS.) ....**8,000. – 12,000.**
- Vee Jay SR 1062, stereo ("SR 1062" in upper right corner of front cover); blank back cover; with "Love Me Do" and "P.S. I Love You"; black label with coloband, oval Vee Jay logo, 1964 ....**1,250. – 2,500.**

❑   Vee Jay SR 1062, stereo ("SR 1062" in upper right corner of front cover); song titles cover; with "Love Me Do" and "P.S. I Love You"; black label with colorband, oval Vee Jay logo, 1964. BEWARE! This album has been heavily counterfeited! If the words "Introducing the Beatles" are above the center hole of the record, and the words "The Beatles" are below, it is automatically a counterfeit and almost worthless (ILLUS.) .... **5,000. – 8,000.**

□   Vee Jay LP 1062, mono ("LP 1062" in lower right corner of front cover); blank
    back cover; with "Please Please Me" and "Ask Me Why"; black label with coloband,
    oval Vee Jay logo, 1964 (ILLUS.) ....**500.00 – 1,000.**
□   Vee Jay LP 1062, mono ("LP 1062" in lower right corner of front cover); song
    titles cover; with "Please Please Me" and "Ask Me Why"; oval Vee Jay logo with
    colorband, 1964... **150.00 - 300.00**

❑ Vee Jay LP 1062, mono ("LP 1062" in lower right corner of front cover); song
titles cover; with "Please Please Me" and "Ask Me Why"; brackets Vee Jay logo with
colorband (most common authentic version), 1964

(ILLUS.) .... **125.00 - 250.00**

❑ Vee Jay LP 1062, mono ("LP 1062" in lower right corner of front cover); song titles
cover; with "Please Please Me" and "Ask Me Why"; oval Vee Jay logo on solid black
label, 1964.. **150.00 - 300.00**

- ❏ Vee Jay LP 1062, mono ("LP 1062" in lower right corner of front cover); song titles cover; with "Please Please Me" and "Ask Me Why"; plain Vee Jay logo on solid black label, 1964 (ILLUS.) .... **125.00 - 250.00**
- ❏ Vee Jay LP 1062, mono ("LP 1062" in lower right corner of front cover); song titles cover; with "Please Please Me" and "Ask Me Why"; brackets Vee Jay logo on solid black label, authentic copies have a small Vee-Jay logo, counterfeits have a large Vee-Jay logo, 1964 .... **500.00 – 1,000.**
- ❏ Vee Jay LP 1062, mono ("LP 1062" in lower right corner of front cover); with "Please Please Me" and "Ask Me Why"; back cover has the "new" song titles cover pasted over the "old" song titles cover, 1964 .... **500.00 – 1,000.**

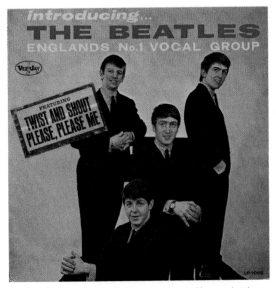

❏ Vee Jay LP 1062, mono ("LP 1062" in lower right corner of front cover); with "Please Please Me" and "Ask Me Why"; with sticker on cover stating "Featuring Twist and Shout//Please, Please Me," 1964 (ILLUS.) .... **300.00 - 600.00**

❏ Vee Jay SR 1062, stereo ("SR 1062" in upper right corner of front cover, or white "Stereophonic" or foil "Stereo" sticker at lower left), song titles cover; with "Please Please Me" and "Ask Me Why"; oval Vee Jay logo with colorband, 1964 .... **400.00 – 1,600.**

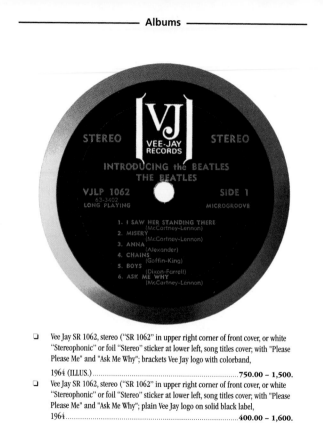

❑ Vee Jay SR 1062, stereo ("SR 1062" in upper right corner of front cover, or white "Stereophonic" or foil "Stereo" sticker at lower left, song titles cover; with "Please Please Me" and "Ask Me Why"; brackets Vee Jay logo with colorband,

1964 (ILLUS.) ....**750.00 – 1,500.**

❑ Vee Jay SR 1062, stereo ("SR 1062" in upper right corner of front cover, or white "Stereophonic" or foil "Stereo" sticker at lower left, song titles cover; with "Please Please Me" and "Ask Me Why"; plain Vee Jay logo on solid black label,

1964 ....**400.00 – 1,600.**

INTRODUCING THE BEATLES (FAKES)

The stereo version of *Introducing the Beatles* may be the most counterfeited album of all time. From 1965 until the 1980s, fake copies of this album flooded bargain bins at respectable record stores and department stores. With real copies so valuable, it's no wonder that the average record accumulator wants to think they have something "rare" when the item is nothing more than fool's gold.. Therefore, here are some photos of obvious fake copies.

If there is a brown border around the outside cover, it's a fake.

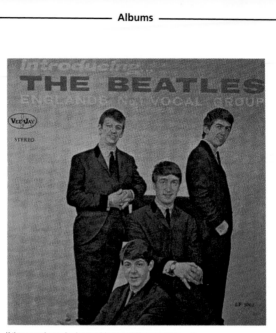

If the cover is washed out or blurry, or if the word "Stereo" appears under the "Vee Jay" logo, or George Harrison's shadow is missing, it's a fake.

LEGITIMATE   COUNTERFEIT

Many pirated covers were well reproduced and "look" real.
Another identification method is to look at the word
"HONEY" in the song title "A TASTE OF HONEY";
if any pieces of the letters "H" and "E" are missing,
it's a fake.

At first glance, this label looks real. But look closely: The color green is missing from the colorband. Therefore, it's fake.

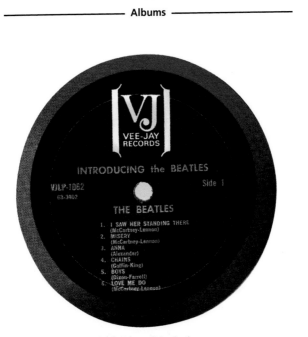

This label looks more real at first glance. But notice the placement of the words "THE BEATLES" on the label. *With NO EXCEPTIONS, any copy of* Introducing the Beatles *where the words "THE BEATLES" are below the center hole is a counterfeit!* This is regardless of what the cover looks like.

JOLLY WHAT! THE BEATLES AND FRANK IFIELD ON STAGE

Also see THE BEATLES AND FRANK IFIELD ON STAGE.

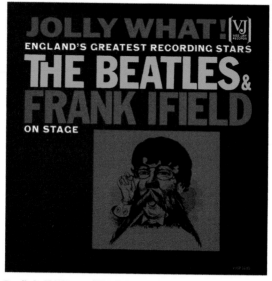

❑ Vee Jay LP 1085, mono ("VJLP 1085" at lower right front cover), man in Beatle wig cover; originals have printing on spine and a dark blue/purple background; counterfeits have a black background and no spine print; oval Vee Jay logo with colorband 1964 (ILLUS.) .... **125.00 - 250.00**

❑ Vee Jay LP 1085, mono ("VJLP 1085" at lower right front cover), man in Beatle wig cover; originals have printing on spine and a dark blue/purple background; counterfeits have a black background and no spine print; brackets Vee Jay logo with colorband, 1964 .... **125.00 - 250.00**

❑ Vee Jay LP 1085, mono ("VJLP 1085" at lower right front cover), man in Beatle wig cover; originals have printing on spine and a dark blue/purple background; counterfeits have a black background and no spine print; plain Vee Jay logo on solid black label, most known counterfeits have this label, 1964 .... **125.00 - 250.00**

❑ Vee Jay SR 1085, stereo ("STEREO" at center top front cover), man in Beatle wig cover; originals have printing on spine, a dark blue/purple background and "STEREO" at top of cover; counterfeits have a black background, no spine print and "STEREO" at lower right front cover; oval Vee Jay logo with colorband, 1964 .... **250.00 - 500.00**

❑ Vee Jay SR 1085, stereo ("STEREO" at center top front cover), man in Beatle wig cover; originals have printing on spine, a dark blue/purple background and "STEREO" at top of cover; counterfeits have a black background, no spine print and "STEREO" at lower right front cover; brackets Vee Jay logo with colorband, 1964 .... **250.00 - 500.00**

❑ Vee Jay SR 1085, stereo ("STEREO" at center top front cover), man in Beatle wig cover; originals have printing on spine, a dark blue/purple background and "STEREO" at top of cover; counterfeits have a black background, no spine print and "STEREO" at lower right front cover; plain Vee Jay on solid black label, 1964 .... **250.00 - 500.00**

❑ Vee Jay LP or SR 1085, any counterfeit version ....**2.00 – 8.00**

LET IT BE

- ❏ Apple AR-34001, red Apple label; authentic copies have "Bell Sound" stamped in trail-off area and the initials "SF," though because of the many copies pressed at the same time, they may be faint; counterfeit copies, which flooded the market in the mid-1970s, do not have "Bell Sound" in the trail-off and have blurry reproduction of both the Apple label and the covers; these counterfeits have no collector value, 1970 (ILLUS.) .... **12.50 - 25.00**

❑ Capitol SW-11922, purple label, large Capitol logo; with poster and custom innersleeve, 1979 .... **7.50 - 15.00**

❑ Capitol SW-11922, black label, print in colorband; add 33% if poster is included, 1983 .... **7.50 - 15.00**

❑ Mobile Fidelity 1-109, "Original Master Recording" on front cover; gatefold, 1987 . **20.00 - 40.00**

❑ Mobile Fidelity 1-109, "Original Master Recording" on front cover; non-gatefold cover, 1987 .... **100.00 - 200.00**

❑ Capitol SW-11922, purple label, small Capitol logo; add 20% if poster and custom innersleeve are included, 1988 .... **12.50 - 25.00**

❑ Capitol C1-46447, new number (the only 1995 reissue with a completely new number), 1995 .... **6.00 - 12.00**

LIGHTNING STRIKES TWICE

❑ United Distributors UDL-2382 [M], Side 1 has five Beatles' Decca audition tracks; Side 2 has live Elvis Presley performances from 1955, 1981 .... **30.00 - 60.00**

LIKE DREAMERS DO

❑ Backstage 2-201, 2-record set, gatefold package, individually numbered (numbers under 100 increase value significantly), 1982 .... **20.00 - 40.00**

❑ Backstage 2-201, 2-record set, non-gatefold package, 1982 .... **25.00 - 50.00**

❑ Backstage BSR-1111, gray vinyl promo in white sleeve, 1982 .... **25.00 - 50.00**

❑ Backstage BSR-1111, white vinyl promo in white sleeve, 1982 .... **25.00 - 50.00**

❑ Backstage BSR-1111, 3-record set, contains two picture discs with 10 of the Decca audition tracks on one, interviews on the other, plus one white-vinyl record with the same contests as the musical picture disc, 1982 .... **30.00 - 60.00**

❑ Backstage BSR-1111, 3-record set, contains two picture discs with 10 of the Decca audition tracks on one, interviews on the other, plus one gray-vinyl record with the same contests as the musical picture disc, 1982 .... **50.00 - 100.00**

LIVE 1962, HAMBURG, GERMANY

❏ Hall of Music HM-1-2200, 2-record set, this is the only American LP with the original Eurpoean contents -- "I Saw Her Standing There," "Twist and Shout," "Ask Me Why" and "Reminiscing" replace the four songs listed with the Lingasong issue, 1981 .... **25.00 - 50.00**

LIVE AT THE BBC

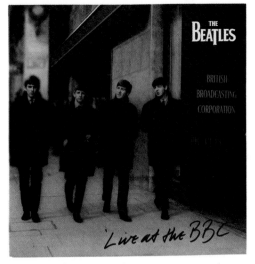

❏ Apple C1-8-31796, two-record set, only 25,000 U.S. copies were pressed, 1994 (ILLUS.) .... **25.00 - 50.00**

LIVE AT THE STAR CLUB IN HAMBURG, GERMANY, 1962

❏ Lingasong LS-2-7001, 2-record set, promo only on red vinyl, 1977 .... **100.00 - 200.00**

❏ Lingasong LS-2-7001, 2-record set, promo only on blue vinyl, 1977 .... **150.00 - 300.00**

❏ Lingasong LS-2-7001, 2-record set, promo on black vinyl; "D.J. Copy Not for Sale" on labels, 1977 .... **20.00 - 40.00**

❏ Lingasong LS-2-7001, 2-record set, this version contains "I'm Gonna Sit Right Down and Cry," "Where Have You Been All My Life," "Till There Was You," and "Sheila," which are not on imports, 1977 .... **10.00 - 20.00**

LOVE SONGS

❏ Capitol SKBL-11711, two-record set, with booklet and embossed, leather-like cover, 1977 .... **10.00 - 20.00**

❏ Capitol SKBL-11711, two-record set, with booklet, but without embossed cover, 1988 .... **15.00 - 30.00**

MAGICAL MYSTERY TOUR

❏ Capitol MAL 2835, mono, black label with colorband; with 24-page book bound
into center of gatefold; all mono copies have every song credited to "BMI" on both
sides, 1967 (ILLUS.) .... **150.00 - 300.00**

❑ Capitol SMAL 2835, stereo, black label with colorband; with 24-page booklet bound into center of gatefold; original copies have "BMI" credit after every song on label and "All selections are published by Maclen Music, Inc., BMI" on left inside gatefold, 1967 (ILLUS.) .... **75.00 - 150.00**

❑ Capitol SMAL 2835, stereo, black label with colorband; with 24-page booklet bound into center of gatefold; second pressings have "ASCAP" credit after every song on Side 1 label and "All side-one selections are published by Comet Music Corp, ASCAP" under side-1 titles on left inside gatefold, 1967............... **60.00 - 120.00**

❑   Capitol SMAL 2835, stereo, black colorband label; border print adds "A Subsidiary of Capitol Industries Inc."; with 24-page booklet, 1968 (ILLUS.) .... **30.00 - 60.00**

❏ Capitol SMAL 2835, stereo, lime green label; with 24-page booklet,
   1969 .... **25.00 - 50.00**
❏ Apple/Capitol SMAL 2835, stereo, Apple label with Capitol logo on Side 2 bottom;
   cover still says "Capitol"; with 24- page booklet, 1971 .... **20.00 - 40.00**
❏ Apple/Capitol SMAL 2835, stereo, with "Mfd. by Apple" on label; cover still says
   "Capitol," with 24-page booklet, 1971 .... **10.00 - 20.00**
❏ Apple/Capitol SMAL 2835, stereo, Apple label with "All Rights Reserved" on label;
   cover still says "Capitol"; with 24- page booklet, 1975 .... **12.50 - 25.00**
❏ Capitol SMAL 2835, stereo, orange label; with 24-page booklet,
   1976 .... **6.00 - 12.00**
❏ Capitol SMAL 2835, stereo, purple label, large Capitol logo; this edition did not
   come with booklet, 1978 .... **5.00 - 10.00**
❏ Mobile Fidelity 1-047, stereo, "Original Master Recording" on top of front cover,
   1980 .... **30.00 - 60.00**
❏ Capitol SMAL 2835, stereo, black label, print in colorband; no booklet,
   1983 .... **7.50 - 15.00**
❏ Capitol C1-48062, stereo, new number; purple label, small Capitol logo; no booklet,
   1988 .... **12.50 - 25.00**
❏ Capitol C1-48062, stereo, with Apple logo on back cover; reissue restores booklet to
   package, 1995 .... **6.00 - 12.00**

MEET THE BEATLES!

❑   Capitol T 2047, mono, black label with colorband; "Beatles!" on cover in tan to brown print; "ASCAP" and "BMI" credits are missing on the label; no producer credit on back cover; this is the first edition of the LP, 1964 (ILLUS.) .... **200.00 - 400.00**

❑   Capitol T 2047, mono, black label with colorband; "Beatles!" on cover in tan to brown print; label has "ASCAP" after every title except "I Want to Hold Your Hand" (BMI); no producer credit on back cover; this is the second edition of the LP, 1964 (ILLUS.) .... **100.00 - 200.00**

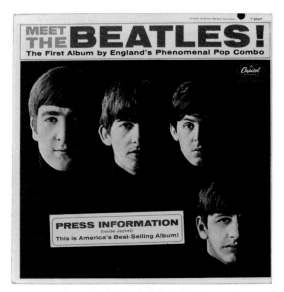

❑ Capitol T 2047, mono, black label with colorband; "Beatles!" on cover in tan
to brown print; no producer credit on back cover; yellow sticker on lower left
front cover that states "PRESS INFORMATION (Inside Jacket) This Is America's
Best-Selling Album!"; this version was given to media members who attended a
February 10, 1964 conference at the Plaza Hotel in New York; a complete package
contains two glossy photos, five pages of biography, and a copy of the "National
Record News"; price is for cover and record without extra materials,

1964 (ILLUS.) ....**3,000.00 – 4,000.00**

☐ Capitol T 2047, mono, black label with colorband; "Beatles!" on cover in tan to brown print; some labels have "ASCAP" after every title except "I Want to Hold Your Hand"; other labels have "ASCAP" after every title except "I Want to Hold Your Hand," "I Saw Her Standing There" and "I Wanna Be Your Man"; still other labels have "ASCAP" after every title except "I Want to Hold Your Hand" and "I Wanna Be Your Man"; most of the back covers add "Produced by George Martin" to lower left, 1964 (ILLUS.) ....**75.00 - 150.00**

☐ Capitol T 2047, mono, black label with colorband; "Beatles!" on cover in green print; many of these have a label giving "BMI" credit to every song except "Don't Bother Me" and "Till There Was You"; most of these have "Produced by George Martin" on lower left of back cover, 1965 ....**50.00 - 100.00**

❑ Capitol ST 2047, stereo, black label with colorband; "Beatles!" on cover in tan to brown print; "ASCAP" and "BMI" credits are missing on the label; no producer credit on back cover; this is the first edition of the LP, 1964 ...... **200.00 - 400.00**

❑ Capitol ST 2047, stereo, black label with colorband; "Beatles!" on cover in tan to brown print; label has "ASCAP" after every title except "I Want to Hold Your Hand" (BMI); no producer credit on back cover; this is the second edition of this LP, 1964 (ILLUS.) ....**75.00 - 150.00**

❑ Capitol ST 2047, stereo, black label with colorband; "Beatles!" on cover in tan to brown print; some labels have "ASCAP" after every title except "I Want to Hold Your Hand"; other labels have "ASCAP" after every title except "I Want to Hold Your Hand," "I Saw Her Standing There" and "I Wanna Be Your Man"; still other labels have "ASCAP" after every title except "I Want to Hold Your Hand" and "I Wanna Be Your Man"; back cover adds "Produced by George Martin" to lower left, 1964...**60.00 - 120.00**

❑   Capitol ST 2047, stereo, black label with colorband; "Beatles!" on cover in green print; most of these have "Produced by George Martin" on lower left of back cover; many of these have a label giving "BMI" credit to every song except "Don't Bother Me" and "Till There Was You", 1965 (ILLUS.) .... **37.50 - 75.00**

❑   Capitol ST 2047, stereo, black colorband label; border print adds "A Subsidiary of Capitol Industries Inc."; most of these have "GOLD RECORD AWARD" seal added to front cover, 1968 .... **25.00 - 50.00**

- ❏ Capitol ST 2047, stereo, lime green label, 1969 .... **20.00 - 40.00**
- ❏ Capitol ST-8-2047, stereo, Capitol Record Club edition; black label with colorband, 1969 .... **250.00 - 500.00**
- ❏ Capitol ST-8-2047, stereo, Capitol Record Club edition; lime green label, 1969 .... **100.00 - 200.00**
- ❏ Apple/Capitol ST 2047, stereo, Apple label with Capitol logo on Side 2 bottom, cover still says "Capitol," 1971 .... **20.00 - 40.00**
- ❏ Apple/Capitol ST 2047, stereo, with "Mfd. by Apple" on label, cover still says "Capitol," 1971 .... **10.00 - 20.00**
- ❏ Apple/Capitol ST 2047, stereo, Apple label with "All Rights Reserved" on label, cover still says "Capitol," 1975 .... **12.50 - 25.00**
- ❏ Capitol ST 2047, stereo, orange label, 1976 .... **6.00 - 12.00**
- ❏ Capitol ST 2047, stereo, purple label, large Capitol logo at top, 1978 .... **5.00 - 10.00**
- ❏ Capitol ST 2047, stereo, black label, print in colorband, 1983 .... **7.50 - 15.00**
- ❏ Capitol C1-90441, stereo, new number; purple label, smaller Capitol logo at top, 1988 .... **12.50 - 25.00**

MOVIEMANIA

- ❏ Cicadelic 1960, 1987 .... **6.00 - 12.00**

1965 TALK ALBUM — ED RUDY WITH NEW U.S. TOUR

- ❏ Radio Pulsebeat News 3, "The Beatles" in black print under front cover photo (other versions appear to be bootlegs), 1965 .... **75.00 - 150.00**

NOT A SECOND TIME

- ❏ Cicadelic 1961, 1987 .... **6.00 - 12.00**

THE ORIGINAL GREATEST HITS

❑ Greatest GRC-1001, mono, yellow label; this was the first Beatles bootleg album, but it is included because it was sold by mainstream "big-box" retailers; its cover makes it look like a record by a sound-alike group, such as The Liverpools or the Manchesters, but this contained the actual Beatles recordings; Capitol quickly found out and had it taken off the market; this also contains the "Ringo on drums" version of "Love Me Do," dubbed from a Canadian 45, which otherwise did not see American release until 1980, 1964 .... **100.00 - 200.00**

PAST MASTERS VOLUME 1 AND 2

❑ Capitol C1-91135, two-record set, 1988 .... **12.50 - 25.00**

PLEASE PLEASE ME

❑ Mobile Fidelity 1-101, stereo, "Original Master Recording" at top of front cover, British version of album, 1986 .... **20.00 - 40.00**
❑ Capitol CLJ-46435, mono, black label, print in colorband; first Capitol version of original British LP, 1987 .... **10.00 - 20.00**
❑ Capitol CLJ-46435, mono, purple label, small Capitol logo, 1988 .... **12.50 - 25.00**
❑ Capitol C1-46435, mono, new prefix; Apple logo on back cover, 1995 .... **6.00 - 12.00**

RARITIES

❑ Capitol SPRO-8969, purple label, large Capitol logo; part of the U.S. box set The Beatles Collection (BC-13), 1978 .... **25.00 - 50.00**
❑ Capitol SN-12009, promo only, green label; withdrawn before official release; all known copies have a plain white sleeve, 1979 .... **150.00 - 300.00**

❑ Capitol SHAL-12060, mono and stereo, black label with colorband; first pressing has several errors on the back cover notes, as it claims that "There's a Place" was making its stereo debut (it first appeared in stereo in the U.S. on Introducing the Beatles) and that the screaming at the end of "Helter Skelter" was a "classic Lennon statement" (it's actually Ringo), 1980 .... **10.00 - 20.00**

❑ Capitol SHAL-12060, mono and stereo, black label with colorband; with errors deleted and "Produced by George Martin" added to back cover, 1980 .... **7.50 - 15.00**

RECORDED LIVE IN HAMBURG, VOL. 1

❑ Pickwick BAN-90051, mono, 1978 .... **15.00 - 30.00**

RECORDED LIVE IN HAMBURG, VOL. 2

❑ Pickwick BAN-90061, mono, 1978 .... **15.00 - 30.00**

RECORDED LIVE IN HAMBURG, VOL. 3

❑ Pickwick BAN-90071, mono, 1978 .... **20.00 - 40.00**

REEL MUSIC

❑ Capitol SV-12199, yellow vinyl promo; plain white cover, 12-page booklet enclosed, 1982 .... **10.00 - 20.00**

❑ Capitol SV-12199, yellow vinyl promo; numbered back cover with 12-page booklet enclosed, 1982 .... **20.00 - 40.00**

❑ Capitol SV-12199, black vinyl, standard issue, 12-page booklet enclosed, 1982 .... **5.00 - 10.00**

REVOLVER

❑ Capitol T 2576, mono, black label with colorband, early pressings have "Lennon-McCartney" credits on the label for songs they wrote, 1966 ...... **100.00 - 200.00**

❑ Capitol T 2576, mono, black label with colorband, later pressings have "John Lennon-Paul McCartney" credits on the label for songs they wrote, 1966 ....**75.00 - 150.00**

❏   Capitol ST 2576, stereo, black label with colorband, early pressings have "Lennon-McCartney" credits on the label for songs they wrote, 1966 ....**50.00 - 100.00**

❏ Capitol ST 2576, stereo, black label with colorband, later pressings have "John Lennon-Paul McCartney" credits on the label for songs they wrote, 1966 (ILLUS.) .... **40.00 - 80.00**

❑ Capitol ST 2576, stereo, black colorband label; border print adds "A Subsidiary of Capitol Industries Inc.," 1968..**25.00 - 50.00**

❑ Capitol ST 2576, stereo, lime green label, 1969 ....**20.00 - 40.00**

❑ Capitol ST-8-2576, stereo, Capitol Record Club edition; black label with colorband, 1969..**200.00 - 400.00**

❑ Capitol ST-8-2576, stereo, Capitol Record Club edition; lime green label, 1969..**60.00 - 120.00**

❑ Capitol ST 2576, stereo, red label with "target" Capitol at top; same design as lime green label; the only Beatles album known to exist with this label, 1970..**150.00 - 300.00**

❑ Apple/Capitol ST 2576, stereo, Apple label with Capitol logo on Side 2 bottom, cover still says "Capitol," 1971 ....**20.00 - 40.00**

❑ Apple/Capitol ST 2576, stereo, with "Mfd. by Apple" on label, cover still says "Capitol," 1971 ....**10.00 - 20.00**

❑ Capitol ST-8-2576, stereo, Longines Symphonette edition; orange label WITHOUT "All Rights Reserved" on label, 1973 ....**100.00 - 200.00**

❑ Apple/Capitol ST 2576, stereo, Apple label with "All Rights Reserved" on label, cover still says "Capitol," 1975 ....**12.50 - 25.00**

❑ Capitol ST 2576, stereo, orange label with "All Rights Reserved" on label, 1976..**6.00 - 12.00**

❑ Capitol SW 2576, stereo, purple label, large Capitol logo on top, 1978..**5.00 - 10.00**

❑ Capitol SW 2576, stereo, black label, print in colorband, 1983 ....**7.50 - 15.00**

❑ Mobile Fidelity 1-107, stereo, "Original Master Recording" on top of cover, British version of album, 1986 ....**20.00 - 40.00**

❑ Capitol CLJ-46441, stereo, black label, print in colorband; first Capitol version of original British LP, 1987..**10.00 - 20.00**

❑ Capitol CLJ-46441, stereo, British version of album; purple label, small Capitol logo at top, 1988 ....**12.50 - 25.00**

❏ Capitol C1-90452, stereo, new number for American version; purple label, small
Capitol logo at top, 1988 .... **12.50 - 25.00**

❏ Capitol C1-46441, stereo, new prefix; Apple logo on back cover,
1995 .... **6.00 - 12.00**

ROCK 'N' ROLL MUSIC

❏ Capitol SKBO-11537, 2-record set, custom orange labels with Coke glasses,
1976 .... **12.50 - 25.00**

ROCK 'N' ROLL MUSIC, VOLUME 1

❏ Capitol SN-16020, 1980 .... **5.00 - 10.00**

ROCK 'N' ROLL MUSIC, VOLUME 2

❏ Capitol SN-16021, 1980 .... **5.00 - 10.00**

ROUND THE WORLD

❏ Cicadelic 1965, 1986 .... **6.00 - 12.00**

RUBBER SOUL

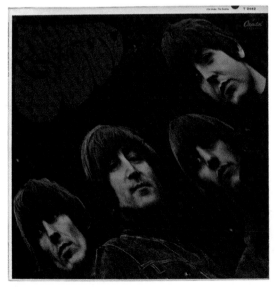

❑ Capitol T 2442, mono, black label with colorband; first edition, without the words "The Beatles" on the label, 1965 (ILLUS.) ....**75.00 - 150.00**
❑ Capitol T 2442, mono, black label with colorband; second edition, with the words "The Beatles" on the label, 1966 ....**60.00 - 120.00**

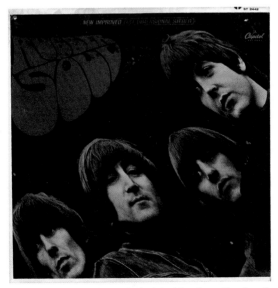

❏ Capitol ST 2442, stereo, black label with colorband; first edition, without the words
"The Beatles" on the label; cover has "New Improved Full Dimensional Stereo" in
brown and no "File Under: The Beatles" at top, 1965 (ILLUS.) ..... **50.00 - 100.00**

❏ Capitol ST 2442, stereo, black label with colorband; with the words "The Beatles"
on the label; cover has "New Improved Full Dimensional Stereo" in black and "File
Under: The Beatles" at top, 1966 .... **40.00 - 80.00**

❑ Capitol ST 2442, stereo, black label with colorband; with the words "The Beatles" on the label; cover has "New Improved Full Dimensional Stereo" twice, in black AND brown, plus "File Under: The Beatles" at top, 1966

(ILLUS.) .... **40.00 - 80.00**

- ❑ Capitol ST 2442, stereo, black colorband label; border print adds "A Subsidiary of Capitol Industries Inc."; initial stereo cover restored, 1968...........**25.00 - 50.00**
- ❑ Capitol ST 2442, stereo, lime green label, 1969 ....**20.00 - 40.00**
- ❑ Capitol ST-8-2442, stereo, Capitol Record Club edition; black label with colorband, 1969 ....**150.00 - 300.00**
- ❑ Capitol ST-8-2442, stereo, Capitol Record Club edition; lime green label, 1969 ....**100.00 - 200.00**
- ❑ Capitol ST-8-2442, stereo, Longines Symphonette edition (will be stated on label); lime green label, 1971 ....**125.00 - 250.00**
- ❑ Apple/Capitol ST 2442, stereo, Apple label with Capitol logo on Side 2 bottom, cover still says "Capitol," 1971 ....**20.00 - 40.00**
- ❑ Apple/Capitol ST 2442, stereo, with "Mfd. by Apple" on label, cover still says "Capitol," 1971 ....**10.00 - 20.00**
- ❑ Apple/Capitol ST 2442, stereo, Apple label with "All Rights Reserved" on label, cover still says "Capitol," 1975 ....**12.50 - 25.00**
- ❑ Capitol ST 2442, stereo, orange label, 1976.............................**6.00 - 12.00**
- ❑ Capitol SW 2442, stereo, purple label, large Capitol logo at top, 1978...**5.00 - 10.00**
- ❑ Capitol SW 2442, stereo, black label, print in colorband, 1983 ....**7.50 - 15.00**
- ❑ Mobile Fidelity 1-106, stereo, "Original Master Recording" at top of front cover, British version of album, 1985 ....**20.00 - 40.00**
- ❑ Capitol CLJ-46440, stereo, black label, print in colorband; first Capitol version of original British LP, 1987...**10.00 - 20.00**
- ❑ Capitol CLJ-46440, stereo, British version of album; purple label, small Capitol logo at top, 1988 ....**12.50 - 25.00**
- ❑ Capitol C1-90453, stereo, new number for American version; purple label, small Capitol logo at top, 1988 ....**12.50 - 25.00**
- ❑ Capitol C1-46440, stereo, new prefix; British version of album; Apple logo on back cover, 1995 ....**6.00 - 12.00**

THE SAVAGE YOUNG BEATLES

❏ Savage BM-69, mono, orange label; no legitimate copy says "Stereo" on
cover, 1964 ....**75.00 - 150.00**

❏ Savage BM-69, mono, yellow label, glossy orange cover,
1964 ....**750.00 – 1,500.**

SGT. PEPPER'S LONELY HEARTS CLUB BAND

❏   Capitol MAS 2653, mono, black label with colorband; first back cover makes no mention of NEMS or Maclen anywhere, first label calls Side 1, Song 2 "A Little Help from My Friends," 1967 (ILLUS.) .... **200.00 - 400.00**

❑ Capitol MAS 2653, mono, black label with colorband; second back cover has "© NEMS Enterprises Ltd, 1967" at lower left; with label that calls Side 1, Song 2 "A Little Help from My Friends," 1967 (ILLUS.) .... 150.00 - 300.00

❑ Capitol MAS 2653, mono, black label with colorband; third back cover has "© NEMS Enterprises Ltd, 1967" at lower right in tiny print above "Manufactured by Capitol Records Inc."; with label that calls Side 1, Song 2 "A Little Help from My Friends," 1967 .... 125.00 - 250.00

❑ Capitol MAS 2653, mono, black label with colorband; fourth back cover has "All rights for the United States, Canada, Mexico and the Philippines controlled by MACLEN MUSIC INC." at lower right above "Manufactured by Capitol Records Inc."; with label that calls Side 1, Song 2 "With a Little Help from My Friends," 1967 (ILLUS.) .... **150.00 - 300.00**

❑ Capitol SMAS 2653, stereo, black label with colorband; first back cover makes no
   mention of NEMS or Maclen anywhere, first label calls Side 1, Song 2 "A Little Help
   from My Friends," 1967 (ILLUS.) ....**60.00 - 120.00**

❑ Capitol SMAS 2653, stereo, black label with colorband; second back cover has "©
   NEMS Enterprises Ltd, 1967" at lower right in tiny print above "Manufactured by
   Capitol Records Inc."; with label that calls Side 1, Song 2 "A Little Help from My
   Friends," 1967 ....**50.00 - 100.00**

❑ Capitol SMAS 2653, stereo, black label with colorband; third back cover has "©
   1967 NEMS – NEMS Enterprises Limited" vertically along lower right edge and
   no mention of Maclen; with label that calls Side 1, Song 2 "A Little Help from My
   Friends," 1967 ....**50.00 - 100.00**

- Capitol SMAS 2653, stereo, black label with colorband; fourth back cover has "All rights for the United States, Canada, Mexico and the Philippines controlled by MACLEN MUSIC INC." at lower right above "Manufactured by Capitol Records Inc."; with label that calls Side 1, Song 2 "With a Little Help from My Friends,"

  1967 (ILLUS.) .... **40.00 - 80.00**

- Capitol SMAS 2653, stereo, black colorband label; border print adds "A Subsidiary of Capitol Industries Inc.", 1968 .... **30.00 - 60.00**
- Capitol SMAS 2653, stereo, lime green label, 1969 .... **25.00 - 50.00**
- Apple/Capitol SMAS 2653, stereo, Apple label with Capitol logo on Side 2 bottom, cover still says "Capitol," 1971 .... **20.00 - 40.00**
- Apple/Capitol SMAS 2653, stereo, with "Mfd. by Apple" on label, cover still says "Capitol," 1971 .... **12.50 - 25.00**
- Apple/Capitol SMAS 2653, stereo, Apple label with "All Rights Reserved" on label, cover still says "Capitol," 1975 .... **12.50 - 25.00**
- Capitol SMAS 2653, stereo, orange label, 1976 .... **6.00 - 12.00**
- Capitol SMAS 2653, stereo, purple label, large Capitol logo on top; many copies from 1978 had a "The Original Classic" sticker on shrink wrap; it was added at the time of the release of the movie version of Sgt. Pepper; double this value if the sticker is still there, 1978 .... **5.00 - 10.00**
- Capitol SEAX-11840, picture disc in die-cut cardboard cover; 250,000 were pressed; deduct 25% if there is a cut-out indicator on cover, 1978 .... **10.00 - 20.00**
- Mobile Fidelity UHQR 1-100, stereo, "Ultra High Quality Recording" release with special cover; numbered edition of 5,000; numbers under 100 fetch even more, 1982 .... **150.00 - 300.00**
- Capitol SMAS 2653, stereo, black label, print in colorband; some of these had "The Original Classic" sticker; add $10 to value if it is there., 1983 .... **7.50 - 15.00**
- Mobile Fidelity 1-100, stereo, "Original Master Recording" at top of front cover, 1985 .... **20.00 - 40.00**
- Capitol C1-46442, stereo, new number; purple label, small Capitol logo at top, 1988 .... **12.50 - 25.00**
- Capitol C1-46442 , stereo, with Apple logo on back cover, 1995 .... **6.00 - 12.00**

SGT. PEPPER'S LONELY HEARTS CLUB BAND
CUT-OUT INSERTS

❑   Capitol 2653, this was available with most, if not all, editions of the LP,
    1967 (ILLUS.) ....1.00 - 3.00

SGT. PEPPER'S LONELY HEARTS CLUB BAND SPECIAL INNER SLEEVE

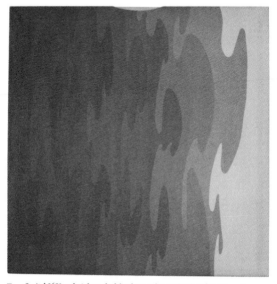

❏ Capitol 2653, red-pink psychedelic sleeve only issued with 1967 editions, also sometimes found with "Magical Mystery Tour" LPs, 1967

(ILLUS.) .... **7.50 - 15.00**

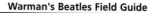

THE SILVER BEATLES

❏ Orange ORC-12880, test pressing; white cover with title sticker,
  1985 .... **150.00 - 300.00**

❏ Orange ORC-12880, test pressing; full cover cover slick folded around a white
  cover, 1985 .... **200.00 - 400.00**

SILVER BEATLES, VOLUME 1

❏ Phoenix PHX-352, mono, contains seven Decca audition tracks,
  1982 .... **6.00 - 12.00**

SILVER BEATLES, VOLUME 2

❏ Phoenix PHX-353, mono, contains seven more Decca audition tracks,
  1982 .... **6.00 - 12.00**

SOMETHING NEW

❏ Capitol T 2108, mono, black label with colorband, with one of the translator's
names misspelled "Nicholas" on "Komm, Gib Mir Deine Hand,"

1964 (ILLUS.) .... **100.00 - 200.00**

❏ Capitol T 2108, mono, black label with colorband, with translator's name correctly

spelled "Nicolas" on "Komm, Gib Mir Deine Hand," 1964 .... **75.00 - 150.00**

❑ Capitol ST 2108, stereo, black label with colorband, with one of the translator's names misspelled "Nicholas" on "Komm, Gib Mir Deine Hand,"

1964 (ILLUS.) ....**60.00 - 120.00**

❏ Capitol ST 2108, stereo, black label with colorband, with translator's name correctly spelled "Nicolas" on "Komm, Gib Mir Deine Hand," 1964 ....**40.00 - 80.00**

❏ Capitol ST 2108, stereo, black colorband label; border print adds "A Subsidiary of Capitol Industries Inc.", 1968 ....**25.00 - 50.00**

❏ Capitol ST 2108, stereo, lime green label, 1969 ....**20.00 - 40.00**

❏ Capitol ST-8-2108, stereo, Capitol Record Club edition; black label with colorband, 1969 ....**150.00 - 300.00**

❏ Capitol ST-8-2108, stereo, Capitol Record Club edition; lime green label, 1969 ....**75.00 - 150.00**

❏ Capitol ST-8-2108, stereo, Longines Symphonette edition (will be stated on label); lime green label, 1971 ....**150.00 - 300.00**

❏ Apple/Capitol ST 2108, stereo, Apple label with Capitol logo on Side 2 bottom, cover still says "Capitol," 1971 ....**20.00 - 40.00**

❏ Apple/Capitol ST 2108, stereo, with "Mfd. by Apple" on label, cover still says "Capitol," 1971 ....**10.00 - 20.00**

❏ Apple/Capitol ST 2108, stereo, Apple label with "All Rights Reserved" on label, cover still says "Capitol," 1975 ....**12.50 - 25.00**

❏ Capitol ST 2108, stereo, orange label, 1976 ....**6.00 - 12.00**

❏ Capitol ST 2108, stereo, purple label, large Capitol logo at top, 1978 ....**5.00 - 10.00**

❏ Capitol ST 2108, stereo, black label, print in colorband, 1983 ....**7.50 - 15.00**

❏ Capitol C1-90443, stereo, new number; purple label, small Capitol logo at top, 1988 ....**12.50 - 25.00**

SONGS AND PICTURES OF THE FABULOUS BEATLES

❏ Vee Jay LP 1092, all copies with this title, regardless of label, are counterfeits ....**2.50 - 5.00**

SONGS, PICTURES AND STORIES OF THE FABULOUS BEATLES

❏ Vee Jay VJ 1092, mono ("VJ 1092" at bottom front), all copies have gatefold cover with 2/3 width on front; all copies have "Introducing the Beatles" records with "1062" numbers; oval Vee Jay logo with colorband.,

1964 (ILLUS.) .... 250.00 - 500.00

❏ Vee Jay VJ 1092, mono ("VJ 1092" at bottom front), all copies have gatefold cover with 2/3 width on front; all copies have "Introducing the Beatles" records with "1062" numbers; brackets Vee Jay logo with colorband, 1964.. **250.00 - 500.00**

❏ Vee Jay VJ 1092, mono ("VJ 1092" at bottom front), all copies have gatefold cover with 2/3 width on front; all copies have "Introducing the Beatles" records with "1062" numbers; oval Vee Jay logo on solid black label, 1964.. **250.00 - 500.00**

❏ Vee Jay VJ 1092, mono ("VJ 1092" at bottom front), all copies have gatefold cover with 2/3 width on front; all copies have "Introducing the Beatles" records with "1062" numbers; plain Vee Jay logo on solid black label, 1964.. **250.00 - 500.00**

❏ Vee Jay VJ 1092, mono ("VJ 1092" at bottom front), with sticker on front cover "Souvenir of Their Appearance at [venue], [city] – [month and date], 1964," 10 different stickers are known to exist, 1964 .... **400.00 - 800.00**

❏ Vee Jay VJS 1092, stereo ("VJS 1092 STEREO" at top or "STEREO" sticker at bottom), all copies have gatefold cover with 2/3 width on front; all copies have "Introducing the Beatles" records with "1062" numbers; oval Vee Jay logo with colorband., 1964.. **1,600.00 – 2,400.**

❏ Vee Jay VJS 1092, stereo ("VJS 1092 STEREO" at top or "STEREO" sticker at bottom), all copies have gatefold cover with 2/3 width on front; all copies have "Introducing the Beatles" records with "1062" numbers; brackets Vee Jay logo with colorband, 1964.. **1,600.00 – 2,400.**

❏ Vee Jay VJS 1092, stereo ("VJS 1092 STEREO" at top or "STEREO" sticker at bottom), all copies have gatefold cover with 2/3 width on front; all copies have "Introducing the Beatles" records with "1062" numbers; plain Vee Jay logo on solid black label, 1964 .... **1,600.00 – 2,400.**

❏ Vee Jay VJS 1092, stereo ("VJS 1092 STEREO" at top or "STEREO" sticker at bottom), with sticker on front cover "Souvenir of Their Appearance at [venue], [city] – [month and date], 1964," 10 different stickers are known to exist, 1964 (ILLUS.) .... **2,500. - 4,000.**

TALK DOWNUNDER

❑ Raven/PVC 8911, 1981 .... **5.00 - 10.00**
❑ Raven/PVC 8911, promo version in white cover with title sticker; label reads "For Radio Play Only," 1981 .... **40.00 - 80.00**

THINGS WE SAID TODAY

❑ Cicadelic 1962, 1986 .... **6.00 - 12.00**

THIS IS WHERE IT STARTED

❑ Metro M-563, mono, reissue of the MGM album The Beatles with Tony Sheridan and Guests with two fewer tracks,
1966 .... **50.00 - 100.00**
❑ Metro MS-563, stereo, in stereo cover, 1966 .... **75.00 - 150.00**
❑ Metro MS-563, stereo, in mono cover with "Stereo" sticker,
1966 .... **100.00 - 200.00**

TIMELESS

❑ Silhouette SM-10004, picture disc with all interviews,
1981 .... **10.00 - 20.00**
❑ Silhouette SM-10004, picture disc with interviews plus remakes of "Imagine" and "Let It Be" by non-Beatles, 1981 .... **12.50 - 25.00**

TIMELESS II

❑ Silhouette SM-10010, picture disc with mostly interviews,
1982 .... **10.00 - 20.00**

20 GREATEST HITS

❑   Capitol SV-12245, stereo, purple label, large Capitol logo at top, "Yesterday" is
listed on labe as running for 1:04, 1982 (ILLUS.) .... **10.00 - 20.00**

❑ Capitol SV-12245, stereo, purple label, large Capitol logo at top, "Yesterday" is listed on lable as running for 2:04, 1982 .... **12.50 - 25.00**

❑ Capitol SV-12245, stereo, black label, print in colorband, 1983 .... **10.00 - 20.00**

❑ Capitol SV-12245, stereo, purple label, small Capitol logo at top, 1988 .... **12.50 - 25.00**

20 HITS, BEATLES

❑ Phoenix P20-623, contains 12 Decca audition tracks, four Beatles/Tony Sheridan tracks, and four Tony Sheridan solo tracks, 1983 .... **10.00 - 20.00**

❑ Phoenix P20-629, with 20 live Hamburg tracks, 1983 .... **10.00 - 20.00**

UNITED ARTISTS PRESENTS A HARD DAY'S NIGHT

❑ United Artists SP-2359/60, promo only, open-end interview with script, 1964 .... **1,500. – 2,000.**

❑ United Artists SP-2362/3, promo only, radio spots for movie, 1964 .... **750.00 – 1,500.**

UNITED ARTISTS PRESENTS HELP!

❑ United Artists UA-Help-INT, promo only, open-end interview with script, red label, 1965 .... **1,500. – 2,000.**

❑ United Artists UA-Help-Show, promo only, one-sided interview with script, blue label, 1965 .... **2,250. – 3,000.**

❑ United Artists UA-Help-A/B, promo only, radio spots for movie, 1965 .... **1,000. - 1.500.**

WEST COAST INVASION

❑ Cicadelic 1966, 1985 .... **6.00 - 12.00**

THE WHITE ALBUM

See THE BEATLES.

WITH THE BEATLES

❏ Mobile Fidelity 1-102, stereo, "Original Master Recording" on top of front cover, British version of album; this record had a more limited run than other Mobile Fidelity Beatles LPs because of a damaged stamper that was not replaced, 1986..**75.00 - 150.00**

❏ Capitol CLJ-46436, mono, black label, print in colorband; first Capitol version of original British LP, 1987...**10.00 - 20.00**

❏ Capitol CLJ-46436, mono, purple label, small Capitol logo at top, 1988...**12.50 - 25.00**

❏ Capitol C1-46436, mono, new prefix; Apple logo on back cover, 1995...**6.00 - 12.00**

YELLOW SUBMARINE

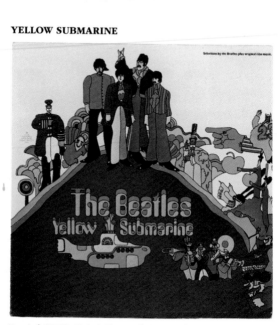

❑   Apple SW-153, with Capitol logo on Side 2 bottom, 1969
     (ILLUS.) ....**25.00 - 50.00**

- ❏ Apple SW-153, with "Mfd. by Apple" on label, 1971.................. **10.00 - 20.00**
- ❏ Apple SW-153, with "All Rights Reserved" on label,
  1975... **12.50 - 25.00**
- ❏ Capitol SW-153, orange label, 1976 .... **6.00 - 12.00**
- ❏ Capitol SW-153, purple label, large Capitol logo, 1978 .... **5.00 - 10.00**
- ❏ Capitol SW-153, black label, print in colorband, 1983 .... **7.50 - 15.00**
- ❏ Mobile Fidelity 1-108, "Original Master Recording" on front cover,
  1987 .... **30.00 - 60.00**
- ❏ Capitol C1-46445, new number; purple label, small Capitol logo,
  1988 .... **12.50 - 25.00**
- ❏ Capitol C1-46445, reissue has the British liner notes, which include a review of the
  "White Album," 1995 .... **6.00 - 12.00**

THE YELLOW SUBMARINE (A UNITED ARTISTS RELEASE)

APPLE FILMS

Presents

"THE YELLOW SUBMARINE"

(A United Artists Release)

33⅓   LP

RADIO SPOTS

CUT 1........0:60
CUT 2........0:60
CUT 3.✛4..0:30
CUT ✗.5....0:10

(KAL 004)

❑ Apple Films KAL 004, one-sided LP with radio spots for movie; all known copies have writing on the label where the times for the spots were corrected; this has no effect on the value of the record, 1969 (ILLUS.) .... **1,000. - 2,000.**

YESTERDAY AND TODAY

❑ Capitol T 2553, mono, "first state" butcher cover (never had other cover on top);
cover will be the same size as other Capitol Beatles LPs and will have no sign of
discoloration or residue from glue; sealed copies can bring 2-3 times the top value
listed, 1966 (ILLUS.) .... **2,000. – 4,000.**

❑ Capitol T 2553, mono, "second state" butcher cover (trunk cover pasted over
original cover), with no attempt made to peel the top LP cover,
1966 .... **500.00 – 1,000.**

❑ Capitol T 2553, mono, "third state" butcher cover (trunk cover removed, leaving
butcher cover intact); cover will be about 3/16-inch narrower than other Capitol
Beatles LPs and will most likely have glue residue; value is highly negotiable
depending upon the success of removing the paste-over,
1966 .... **800.00 – 1,200.**

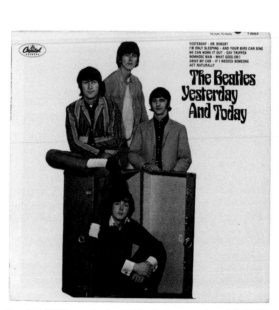

❏ Capitol T 2553, mono, trunk cover with no butcher cover underneath, black label
with colorband, 1966 (ILLUS.) ....**75.00 - 150.00**

❑ Capitol ST 2553, stereo, prototype trunk covers that pre-date the butcher cover; slicks, printer's proofs and/or color separations are known to exist of four different prototypes; these were never used on LPs; unauthorized reproductions exist, 1966 (ILLUS.) .... **3,000. – 4,000.**

❑ Capitol ST 2553, stereo, "first state" butcher cover (never had other cover on top);
cover will be the same size as other Capitol Beatles LPs and will have no sign of
discoloration or residue from glue; sealed copies can bring 3-5 times the top value
listed, 1966 (ILLUS.) .... **6,000 – 8,000.**

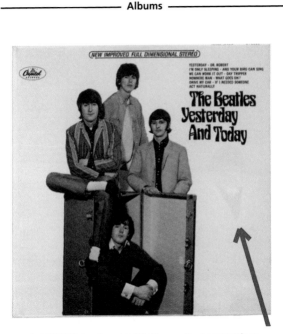

❏ Capitol ST 2553, stereo, "second state" butcher cover (trunk cover pasted over original cover), with no attempt made to peel the top LP cover, 1966 (ILLUS.) ....**750.00 – 2,000.**

❏ Capitol ST 2553, stereo, "third state" butcher cover (trunk cover removed, leaving butcher cover intact); cover will be about 3/16-inch narrower than other Capitol Beatles LPs and will most likely have glue residue; value is highly negotiable depending upon the success of removing the paste-over, 1966 .... **1,000. – 2,500.**

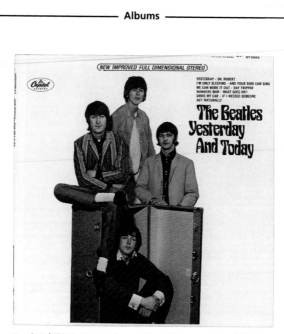

❏ Capitol ST 2553 , stereo, trunk cover with no butcher cover underneath; black label with colorband, 1966 (ILLUS.) .... **40.00 - 80.00**

- ☐ Capitol ST 2553, stereo, trunk cover; most of these have "GOLD RECORD AWARD" seal added to front cover; black colorband label; border print adds "A Subsidiary of Capitol Industries Inc.", 1968 .... **25.00 - 50.00**
- ☐ Capitol ST 2553, stereo, lime green label, 1969 .... **20.00 - 40.00**
- ☐ Capitol ST-8-2553, stereo, Capitol Record Club edition; black label with colorband, 1969 .... **150.00 - 300.00**
- ☐ Capitol ST-8-2553, stereo, Capitol Record Club edition; lime green label, 1969 .... **75.00 - 150.00**
- ☐ Apple/Capitol ST 2553, stereo, Apple label with Capitol logo on Side 2 bottom, covers still say "Capitol," 1971 .... **20.00 - 40.00**
- ☐ Apple/Capitol ST 2553, stereo, with "Mfd. by Apple" on label, covers still say "Capitol," 1971 .... **10.00 - 20.00**
- ☐ Apple/Capitol ST 2553, stereo, Apple label with "All Rights Reserved" on label, covers still say "Capitol," 1975 .... **12.50 - 25.00**
- ☐ Capitol ST 2553, stereo, orange label, 1976 .... **6.00 - 12.00**
- ☐ Capitol ST 2553, stereo, purple label, large Capitol logo at top, 1978 .... **5.00 - 10.00**
- ☐ Capitol ST 2553, stereo, black label, print in colorband, 1983 .... **7.50 - 15.00**
- ☐ Capitol C1-90447, stereo, new number; purple label, small Capitol logo at top, 1988 .... **12.50 - 25.00**

British Singles In Brief

Many of the Beatles' biggest hit singles in the United States were never issued on 45 in England, at least not in the Beatles' 1962-70 heyday. Such songs as "Twist and Shout," "Eight Days a Week," "The Long and Winding Road" and even "Yesterday" were album cuts in the U.K.

Most, but not all, of the Beatles' U.K. singles had the same pairings as the U.S. versions of the same. Sometimes, though, the mix was different, most notably on "I Feel Fine" and "She's a Woman."

It is outside the scope of this book to go into as much detail about the British singles as with the American singles. Please note that *many different label variations exist* with the British records, just as is true with the U.S. editions. **Most copies of the British singles that are currently in the United States are 1970s and 1980s reissues, and most of them fetch only a bit more – and sometimes less – than the American issues from the same time periods.**

All Beatles 45s until 1967, and some later than that, were issued with a punch-out center, as opposed to the American large hole. If this center is missing, the value drops by about half.

Here are the original British Parlophone and Apple singles from 1962 to 1970, and the approximate value of an original edition, in Very Good Plus to Near Mint condition.

Basic Reissue Identification

- Singles with an "EMI" boxed logo on them are reissues from the 1970s and later.
- Only two original Beatles U.K. singles were issued with picture sleeves. Singles with green title/picture sleeves are 1976 reissues. With their sleeves, they are worth $5-$10 each.
- Picture disc singles are 20th anniversary reissues, from 1982 through 1990. These have been increasing in value; they get $15-$25 each, except for "She Loves You" and "A Hard Day's Night," which were much more limited and get $50-$60.
- Singles originally issued in 1962, 1963 or 1964 that have (P) in a circle followed by the release year are reissues.
- A mono single that says "MONO" on the label is a reissue.

ALL YOU NEED IS LOVE/BABY, YOU'RE A RICH MAN

❑ Parlophone R 5620; black label, silver print; exists with both punch-out center inserts or solid centers (value is equal); "Sold in U.K. subject to resale price conditions, see price lists" in center; (P) 1967 toward lower left; perimeter print begins with the words "THE GRAMOPHONE CO. LTD.," first editions do NOT say "(Recorded during 'Live' World Television Transmission)" on them, 1967

....**50.00 - 100.00**

❑ Parlophone R 5620; same as above, except second editions say "(Recorded during 'Live' World Television Transmission)" on them, 1967................. **10.00 - 20.00**

THE BALLAD OF JOHN AND YOKO/OLD BROWN SHOE

❑ Apple R 5786; exists with both punch-out center inserts or solid centers (value is equal); "Sold in U.K. subject to resale price conditions, see price lists" in center; (P) 1969 at left, 1969..**12.50 - 25.00**

CAN'T BUY ME LOVE/YOU CAN'T DO THAT

❑ Parlophone R 5114; black label, silver print; punch-out center intact; "Sold in U.K. subject to resale price conditions, see price lists" in center; "Recording first published 1964" toward lower left; perimeter print begins with the words "THE PARLOPHONE CO. LTD.," 1964 .... **10.00 - 20.00**

FROM ME TO YOU/THANK YOU GIRL

❑ Parlophone R 5015; black label, silver print; punch-out center intact; does NOT state "Sold in U.K. subject to resale price conditions, see price lists"; "Recording first published 1963" toward lower left; perimeter print begins with the words "The Parlophone Co. Ltd.," 1963 .... **12.50 - 25.00**

GET BACK/DON'T LET ME DOWN

❑ Apple R 5777; exists with both punch-out center inserts or solid centers (value is equal); "Sold in U.K. subject to resale price conditions, see price lists" in center; (P) 1969 at left, 1969 .... **12.50 - 25.00**

A HARD DAY'S NIGHT/THINGS WE SAID TODAY

❑ Parlophone R 5160; black label, silver print; punch-out center intact; "Sold in U.K. subject to resale price conditions, see price lists" in center; "Recording first published 1964" toward lower left; perimeter print begins with the words "The Parlophone Co., Ltd.," 1964 .... **10.00 - 20.00**

HELLO GOODBYE/I AM THE WALRUS

❑ Parlophone R 5655; black label, silver print; exists with both punch-out center inserts or solid centers (value is equal); "Sold in U.K. subject to resale price conditions, see price lists" in center; (P) 1967 toward lower left; perimeter print begins with the words "THE GRAMOPHONE CO. LTD.," 1967 .... **12.50 - 25.00**

HELP!/I'M DOWN

❑ Parlophone R 5305; black label, silver print; punch-out center intact; "Sold in U.K. subject to resale price conditions, see price lists" in center; (P) 1965 toward lower left; perimeter print begins with the words "THE PARLOPHONE CO. LTD.," 1965 .... **15.00 - 30.00**

HEY JUDE/REVOLUTION

❑ Apple R 5722; exists with both punch-out center inserts or solid centers (value is equal); "Sold in U.K. subject to resale price conditions, see price lists" in center; (P) 1968 at left, 1968 .... **15.00 - 30.00**

I FEEL FINE/SHE'S A WOMAN

❑ Parlophone R 5200; black label, silver print; punch-out center intact; "Sold in U.K. subject to resale price conditions, see price lists" in center; "Recording first published 1964" toward lower left; perimeter print begins with the words "THE PARLOPHONE CO. LTD.," 1964 ....**10.00 - 20.00**

I WANT TO HOLD YOUR HAND/THIS BOY

❑ Parlophone R 5084; black label, silver print; punch-out center intact; does NOT state "Sold in U.K. subject to resale price conditions, see price lists"; "Recording first published 1963" toward lower left; perimeter print begins with the words "THE PARLOPHONE CO. LTD.," 1963 ....**10.00 - 20.00**

LADY MADONNA/THE INNER LIGHT

❑ Parlophone R 5675; black label, silver print; exists with both punch-out center inserts or solid centers (value is equal); "Sold in U.K. subject to resale price conditions, see price lists" in center; (P) 1968 toward lower left; perimeter print begins with the words "THE GRAMOPHONE CO. LTD.," includes the same basic fan-club insert as the U.S. edition, 1968 ....**50.00 - 100.00**

❑ Parlophone R 5675; same as above, but no insert, 1968 ....**12.50 - 25.00**

LET IT BE/YOU KNOW MY NAME (LOOK UP MY NUMBER)

❑ Apple R 5833; exists with both punch-out center inserts or solid centers (value is equal); (P) 1970 at left, with "APPLES 1002" scratched out in B-side trail-ff area, with picture sleeve (similar to U.S. issue), 1970 ....**40.00 - 80.00**

❑ Apple R 5833; same as above, including "APPLES 1002" trail-off marking, but no picture sleeve, 1970 ....**10.00 - 20.00**

LOVE ME DO/P.S. I LOVE YOU

❏ Parlophone 45-R 4949; red label, silver print; punch-out center intact; does NOT state "Sold in U.K. subject to resale price conditions, see price lists"; "Recording first published 1962" toward lower left; similar 1982 reissues have the word MONO on them, originals do not, 1962 ....**60.00 - 120.00**

PAPERBACK WRITER/RAIN

❏ Parlophone R 5452; black label, silver print; punch-out center intact; "Sold in U.K. subject to resale price conditions, see price lists" in center; (P) 1966 toward lower left; perimeter print begins with the words "THE GRAMOPHONE CO. LTD.," 1966..**15.00 - 30.00**

PLEASE PLEASE ME/ASK ME WHY

❏ Parlophone 45-R 4983; red label, silver print; punch-out center intact; does NOT state "Sold in U.K. subject to resale price conditions, see price lists"; "Recording first published 1963" toward lower left, 1963..............................**75.00 - 150.00**

SHE LOVES YOU/I'LL GET YOU

❏ Parlophone R 5055; black label, silver print; punch-out center intact; does NOT state "Sold in U.K. subject to resale price conditions, see price lists"; "Recording first published 1963" toward lower left; perimeter print begins with the words "The Parlophone Co. Ltd.," 1963 ....**10.00 - 20.00**

SOMETHING/COME TOGETHER

❏ Apple R 5814; exists with both punch-out center inserts or solid centers (value is equal); (P) 1969 at left, 1969..**20.00 - 40.00**

STRAWBERRY FIELDS FOREVER/PENNY LANE

❏ Parlophone R 5570; black label, silver print; punch-out center intact; "Sold in U.K. subject to resale price conditions, see price lists" in center; (P) 1967 toward lower left; perimeter print begins with the words "THE GRAMOPHONE CO. LTD.," with picture sleeve (similar to U.S. issue), 1967..**40.00 - 80.00**

❑ Parlophone R 5570; same as above, without picture sleeve,

1967 ....**12.50 - 25.00**

TICKET TO RIDE/YES IT IS

❑ Parlophone R 5265; black label, silver print; punch-out center intact; "Sold in U.K. subject to resale price conditions, see price lists" in center; (P) 1965 toward lower left; perimeter print begins with the words "THE PARLOPHONE CO. LTD.,"

1965 ....**12.50 - 25.00**

WE CAN WORK IT OUT/DAY TRIPPER

❑ Parlophone R 5289; black label, silver print; punch-out center intact; "Sold in U.K. subject to resale price conditions, see price lists" in center; (P) 1965 toward lower left; perimeter print begins with the words "THE PARLOPHONE CO. LTD.,"

1965 ....**20.00 - 40.00**

YELLOW SUBMARINE/ELEANOR RIGBY

❑ Parlophone R 5493; black label, silver print; punch-out center intact; "Sold in U.K. subject to resale price conditions, see price lists" in center; (P) 1966 toward lower left; perimeter print begins with the words "THE GRAMOPHONE CO. LTD.,"

1966 ....**12.50 - 25.00**

British EPs In Brief

In England, the seven-inch extended play single was much more popular than in the United States. Many collections of Beatles album cuts were issued in this hybrid format, as were at least two collections of all-new material. Perhaps the most famous of these is *Magical Mystery Tour*, which was a two-EP set in the U.K., whereas Capitol in the U.S. added five recent single sides and turned it into a full-length LP.

Many of the physical characteristics of the Parlophone EPs are the same as Parlophone two-song 45s.

Once again, all of the EPs have been reissued, most notably in a 1981 box set called *The Beatles E.P. Collection* (also issued on compact disc in England). All of these have solid center areas, much like those on LPs. The vast majority of originals have punch-out centers. If this center is missing, the value drops by about half. The prices below reflect only *original editions as noted in the descriptions*. Also, they assume that *both the record and cover are there*.

If you have a Parlophone EP that is not listed below, or with the same name but a different number, it was not an English release and is outside the scope of this book.

Here are the original British Parlophone EPs from 1962 to 1967, and the approximate value of an original edition in Very Good Plus to Near Mint condition.

Basic Reissue Identification

- EPs originally issued in 1963 or 1964 that have (P) in a circle followed by the release year are reissues.
- For EPs released from 1964 to 1967, if the words "Sold in U.K. subject to resale price conditions, see price lists" are NOT in the center, it's a reissue.
- All the original Beatles EPs have laminated covers and clear photos. Blurry photos and non-laminated covers are signs of reissues or, in some cases, possibly even counterfeits. Original covers tend to be of much sturdier stock than reissues.

ALL MY LOVING

(Contents: All My Loving/Ask Me Why//Money/P.S. I Love You)

❏ Parlophone GEP 8891, mono, black label, silver and yellow print; punch-out center intact; "Sold in U.K. subject to resale price conditions, see price lists" in center; "Recording first published 1964" at left; perimeter print begins with the words

"THE PARLOPHONE CO. LTD.," 1964 .... **20.00 - 40.00**

THE BEATLES (NO. 1)

(Contents: I Saw Her Standing There/Misery//Anna (Go to Him)/Chains)

❏ Parlophone GEP 8883, mono, black label, silver and yellow print; punch-out center intact; without "Sold in U.K. subject to resale price conditions, see price lists" in center; "Recording first published 1963" at left; perimeter print begins with the words "THE PARLOPHONE CO. LTD.," 1963 .... **25.00 - 50.00**

BEATLES FOR SALE

(Contents: No Reply/I'm a Loser//Rock and Roll Music/Eight Days a Week)

❏ Parlophone GEP 8931, mono, black label, silver and yellow print; punch-out center intact; "Sold in U.K. subject to resale price conditions, see price lists" in center; "(P) 1965" at left; perimeter print begins with the words "THE PARLOPHONE CO. LTD.," 1965 .... **25.00 - 50.00**

BEATLES FOR SALE NO. 2

(Contents: I'll Follow the Sun/Baby's in Black//Words of Love/I Don't Want to Spoil the Party)

❏ Parlophone GEP 8938, mono, black label, silver and yellow print; punch-out center intact; "Sold in U.K. subject to resale price conditions, see price lists" in center; "(P) 1965" at left; perimeter print begins with the words "THE GRAMOPHONE CO. LTD.," 1965 .... **30.00 - 60.00**

THE BEATLES' HITS

(Contents: From Me to You/Thank You Girl//Please Please Me/Love Me Do)

❏ Parlophone GEP 8880, mono, black label, silver and yellow print; punch-out center intact; without "Sold in U.K. subject to resale price lists" in center; deos NOT have "Recording first published 1963" or "(P) 1963" at left; perimeter print begins with the words "THE PARLOPHONE CO. LTD.,"

1963 .... **30.00 - 60.00**

THE BEATLES' MILLION SELLERS

(Contents: She Loves You/I Want to Hold Your Hand//Can't Buy Me Love/I Feel Fine)

❏ Parlophone GEP 8946, mono, black label, silver and yellow print; punch-out center intact; "Sold in U.K. subject to resale price conditions, see price lists" in center; "(P) 1965" at left; perimeter print begins with the words "THE PARLOPHONE CO.

LTD.," with "Golden Discs" as title on label, 1965 .... **25.00 - 50.00**

EXTRACTS FROM THE ALBUM A HARD DAY'S NIGHT

(Contents: Any Time at All/I'll Cry Instead//Things We Said Today/When I Get Home)

❏ Parlophone GEP 8924, mono, black label, silver and yellow print; punch-out center intact; "Sold in U.K. subject to resale price conditions, see price lists" in center; "Recording first published 1964" at left; perimeter print begins with the words

"THE PARLOPHONE CO. LTD.," 1964 .... **40.00 - 80.00**

EXTRACTS FROM THE FILM A HARD DAY'S NIGHT

(Contents: I Should Have Known Better/If I Fell//Tell Me Why/And I Love Her)

❏ Parlophone GEP 8920, mono, black label, silver and yellow print; punch-out center intact; "Sold in U.K. subject to resale price conditions, see price lists" in center; "Recording first published 1964" at left; perimeter print begins with the words

"THE PARLOPHONE CO. LTD.," 1964 .... **25.00 - 50.00**

LONG TALL SALLY

(Contents: Long Tall Sally/I Call Your Name//Slow Down/Matchbox)

❏ Parlophone GEP 8913, mono, black label, silver and yellow print; punch-out center intact; "Sold in U.K. subject to resale price conditions, see price lists" in center; "Recording first published 1964" at left; perimeter print begins with the words

"THE PARLOPHONE CO. LTD.," 1964 .... **20.00 - 40.00**

MAGICAL MYSTERY TOUR

(Contents: Disc 1 – Magical Mystery Tour/Your Mother Should Know//I Am
the Walrus; Disc 2 – The Fool on the Hill/Flying//Blue Jay Way)

❏   Parlophone MMT 1, mono, black labels, silver print; exists with both punch-out
center inserts or solid centers (value is equal); "Sold in U.K. subject to resale price
conditions, see price lists" in center; "(P) 1967" at left; perimeter print begins with
the words "THE GRAMOPHONE CO. LTD.," enclosed lyric sheet is blue (yellow lyric
sheet is a reissue), 1967 (ILLUS.) .... **25.00 - 50.00**

❏ Parlophone SMMT 1, stereo, black labels, silver print; exists with both punch-out center inserts or solid centers (value is equal); "Sold in U.K. subject to resale price conditions, see price lists" in center; "(P) 1967" at left; perimeter print begins with the words "THE GRAMOPHONE CO. LTD.," enclosed lyric sheet is blue (yellow lyric sheet is a reissue), 1967 .... **30.00 - 60.00**

NOWHERE MAN

(Contents: Nowhere Man/Drive My Car//Michelle/You Won't See Me)

❏ Parlophone GEP 8952, mono, black label, silver and yellow print; punch-out center intact; "Sold in U.K. subject to resale price conditions, see price lists" in center; "(P) 1966" at left; perimeter print begins with the words "THE GRAMOPHONE CO. LTD.," 1966 .... **75.00 - 150.00**

TWIST AND SHOUT

(Contents: Twist and Shout/A Taste of Honey//Do You Want to Know a Secret/There's a Place)

❏ Parlophone GEP 8882, mono, black label, silver and yellow print; punch-out center intact; without "Sold in U.K. subject to resale price conditions, see price lists" in center; "Recording first published 1963" at left; perimeter print begins with the words "THE PARLOPHONE CO. LTD.," 1963 .... **25.00 - 50.00**

YESTERDAY

(Contents: Yesterday/Act Naturally//You Like Me Too Much/It's Only Love)

❏ Parlophone GEP 8948, mono, black label, silver and yellow print; punch-out center intact; "Sold in U.K. subject to resale price conditions, see price lists" in center; "(P) 1966" at left; perimeter print begins with the words "THE GRAMOPHONE CO. LTD.," 1966 .... **50.00 - 100.00**

British Albums In Brief

In the 1960s, it was not generally known in the United States that all of the albums before *Sgt. Pepper's Lonely Hearts Club Band* were different than the Beatles' albums in the United Kingdom.

Starting in the 1970s, with the growing availability of imported records in the U.S., more Beatles fans became aware of the disparities between releases in the two countries. Finally, in 1987, with the decision by EMI to release the Beatles' compact discs *only* in the original British configurations, the U.K. albums received official release in the States.

It is outside the scope of this book to go into as much detail about the British albums as we did with the American albums. Please note that *many different label variations exist* with the British records, just as is true with the U.S. editions. **Most copies of the British albums that are currently in the United States are 1970s and 1980s reissues, and most of them fetch only a bit more than the American issues from the same time periods.**

Basic Reissue Identification

- All of the non-gatefold albums except Abbey Road were issued in fully laminated front sleeves with three flaps that were glued to the outside of the back cover. Around 1970, cover design changed so that only two flaps were visible on the back; those are reissues.
- Albums originally issued in 1963 or 1964 that have (P) in a circle followed by the release year are reissues.
- Albums originally issued in 1964 to 1969 that lack the words "Sold in U.K. subject to resale price conditions, see price lists" are reissues.
- Albums with the word "Parlophone" in a box at the top, with nine horizontal lines on either side of the box, and with the word "EMI" only at the bottom of the label, are reissues from 1969-70.
- Albums with the word "Parlophone" in a box at the top, with nine horizontal lines on either side of the box, and with the word "EMI" twice on the label, both at the top and the bottom, are reissues from 1970 and later.
- A Parlophone mono album (PMC prefix) that says "MONO" on the label is a reissue.
- Albums on any color vinyl other than black are reissues.

Abbey Road

(Cover is basically the same as the U.S. issue.)

❑ Apple PCS 7088, stereo; unlike other British albums, even the original covers have their flaps pasted inside the cover, with "Sold in U.K. subject to resale price conditions, see price lists" on label, without "Her Majesty" listed on label, 1969 ....**30.00 - 60.00**

❑ Apple PCS 7088, stereo; same as above, except "Her Majesty" is listed on label, 1969 ....**25.00 - 50.00**

The Beatles

(Also known as, but never actually titled, THE WHITE ALBUM. Similar to U.S. issue except as noted.)

❑ Apple PMC 7067/7068, mono, gatefold cover with number stamped on front cover; inner sleeves are black; records come out from the top of the album rather than the side; with "Sold in U.K. subject to resale price conditions, see price lists" on label; includes four individual photos and large poster (included in value), numbers below 0010000 increase the value significantly, 1968 ....**250.00 - 500.00**

❑ Apple PCS 7067/7068, stereo, gatefold cover with number stamped on front cover; inner sleeves are black; records come out from the top of the album rather than the side; with "Sold in U.K. subject to resale price conditions, see price lists" on label; includes four individual photos and large poster (included in value), numbers below 0010000 increase the value significantly, 1968 ....**125.00 - 250.00**

BEATLES FOR SALE

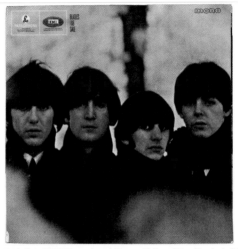

❑ Parlophone PMC 1240, mono, gatefold cover with "mono" in outline (not solid) on
front; label has "Parlophone" standing alone in yellow, with "Sold in U.K. subject
to resale price conditions, see price lists" underneath; "Recording first published
1964" at left; perimeter print begins with the words "THE PARLOPHONE CO. LTD.,"
1964 (ILLUS.) .... **50.00 - 100.00**

❑ Parlophone PCS 3062, stereo, gatefold cover with "stereo" in outline (not solid) on
front; label has "Parlophone" standing alone in yellow, with "Sold in U.K. subject
to resale price conditions, see price lists" underneath; "Recording first published
1964" at left; perimeter print begins with the words "THE PARLOPHONE CO. LTD.,"

1964 .... **75.00 - 150.00**

A COLLECTION OF BEATLES OLDIES

(This album was never issued in the United States.)

❏ Parlophone PMC 7016, mono, label has "Parlophone" standing alone in yellow, with "Sold in U.K. subject to resale price conditions, see price lists" underneath; various (P) dates on label; perimeter print begins with the words "THE GRAMOPHONE CO. LTD.,"1966 (ILLUS.) .... **50.00 - 100.00**

❏ Parlophone PCS 7016, stereo, label has "Parlophone" standing alone in yellow, with "Sold in U.K. subject to resale price conditions, see price lists" underneath; various (P) dates on label; perimeter print begins with the words "THE GRAMOPHONE CO. LTD.," 1966 .... **60.00 - 120.00**

A HARD DAY'S NIGHT

❏ Parlophone PMC 1230, mono, medium-sized "mono" on front; label has "Parlophone" standing alone in yellow, with "Sold in U.K. subject to resale price conditions, see price lists" underneath; "Recording first published 1964" at left; perimeter print begins with the words "THE PARLOPHONE CO. LTD.," 1964 (ILLUS.) .... **50.00 - 100.00**

❏ Parlophone PCS 3058, stereo, medium-sized "stereo" on front; label has "Parlophone" standing alone in yellow, with "Sold in U.K. subject to resale price conditions, see price lists" underneath; "Recording first published 1964" at left; perimeter print begins with the words "THE PARLOPHONE CO. LTD.," 1964 .... **75.00 - 150.00**

HELP!

❑ Parlophone PMC 1255, mono, "mono" in outline (not solid) on front; label has "Parlophone" standing alone in yellow, with "Sold in U.K. subject to resale price conditions, see price lists" underneath; "(P) 1965" at left; perimeter print begins with the words "THE GRAMOPHONE CO. LTD.," 1965 (ILLUS.) .... **50.00 - 100.00**

❑ Parlophone PCS 3071, stereo, "stereo" in outline (not solid) on front; label has "Parlophone" standing alone in yellow, with "Sold in U.K. subject to resale price conditions, see price lists" underneath; "(P) 1965" at left; perimeter print begins with the words "THE GRAMOPHONE CO. LTD.," 1965 .... **60.00 - 120.00**

LET IT BE

(Same music as U.S. edition, but in completely different packaging.)

❑ Apple PXS 1, stereo; box set with record "PCS 7096" in a white sleeve, with Get Back book enclosed in a black tray inside the box; the number "PXS 1" is nowhere on the box or record, 1970 .... **250.00 - 500.00**

❑ Apple PCS 7096, stereo; in standard cover without the box or book, 1970 ....**20.00 - 40.00**

PLEASE PLEASE ME

❑ Parlophone PMC 1202, mono, "Parlophone" in gold outline letters at top, first
edition gives credit to most of the Lennon-McCartney compositions to "Dick James
Mus. Co.," 1963 (ILLUS.)..**400.00 - 800.00**

❑ Parlophone PMC 1202, mono, "Parlophone" in gold outline letters at top, second
edition gives credit to most of the Lennon-McCartney compositions to "Northern
Songs " 1963 ....**350.00 - 700.00**

❑ Parlophone PCS 3042, stereo, "Parlophone" in gold outline letters at top, first edition gives credit to most of the Lennon-McCartney compositions to "Dick James Mus. Co.," 1963 (ILLUS.) ....**2,500. – 4,000.**

❑ Parlophone PCS 3042, stereo, "Parlophone" in gold outline letters at top, second edition gives credit to most of the Lennon-McCartney compositions to "Northern Songs," 1963 ....**2,000. – 3,500.**

REVOLVER

(The UK version has 14 songs, the US version has 11. The US and UK front
cover are similar.)

❏ Parlophone PMC 7009, mono, label has "Parlophone" standing alone in yellow,
with "Sold in U.K. subject to resale price conditions, see price lists" underneath;
"(P) 1966" at left , perimeter print begins with the words "THE GRAMOPHONE CO.
LTD."; with alternate mix of "Tomorrow Never Knows," identifiable by "XEX 606-1"
in trail-off wax, 1966 ....**250.00 – 500.00**

❏ Parlophone PMC 7009, mono, same as above, but with "correct" mix of
"Tomorrow Never Knows," identifiable by "XEX 606-2" or higher in trail-off wax,
1966 ....**75.00 - 150.00**

❏ Parlophone PCS 7009, stereo, label has "Parlophone" standing alone in yellow,
with "Sold in U.K. subject to resale price conditions, see price lists" underneath;
"(P) 1966" at left , perimeter print begins with the words "THE GRAMOPHONE CO.
LTD.," 1966..**75.00 - 150.00**

RUBBER SOUL

(The UK version has 14 songs, the US version has 12. The US and UK front
cover are similar.)

❏ Parlophone PMC 1267, mono, label has "Parlophone" standing alone in yellow,
with "Sold in U.K. subject to resale price conditions, see price lists" underneath;
"(P) 1965" at left , perimeter print begins with the words "THE GRAMOPHONE CO.
LTD."; so-called "loud" mix, identifiable by "XEX 579-1" in trail-off wax,
1965 ....**75.00 - 150.00**

❏ Parlophone PMC 1267, mono, same as above, except "XEX 579-4" or "XEX 579-5"
in trail-off wax, 1965 ....**50.00 - 100.00**

❏ Parlophone PCS 3075, stereo, label has "Parlophone" standing alone in yellow,
with "Sold in U.K. subject to resale price conditions, see price lists" underneath;
"(P) 1965" at left , perimeter print begins with the words "THE GRAMOPHONE CO.
LTD."; 1965..**100.00 - 200.00**

SGT. PEPPER'S LONELY HEARTS CLUB BAND

(Except for some Side 2 trail-off gibberish, this was the first album released
in the U.S. and the U.K. with the same contents.)

❏ Parlophone PMC 7027, mono, label has "Parlophone" standing alone in yellow,
with "Sold in U.K. subject to resale price conditions, see price lists" underneath;
"(P) 1967" at left , perimeter print begins with the words "THE GRAMOPHONE CO.
LTD."; with sheet of cut-outs and original psychedelic red and white inner sleeve;

label mentions "A Day in the Life," 1967 .... **75.00 - 150.00**

❏ Parlophone PMC 7027, mono, same as above except "A Day in the Life" is missing

from Side 2 label, 1967 .... **150.00 - 300.00**

❏ Parlophone PCS 7027, stereo, label has "Parlophone" standing alone in yellow,
with "Sold in U.K. subject to resale price conditions, see price lists" underneath;
"(P) 1967" at left , perimeter print begins with the words "THE GRAMOPHONE CO.
LTD."; with sheet of cut-outs and original psychedelic red and white inner sleeve;

all labels mention "A Day in the Life," 1967 .... **60.00 - 120.00**

WITH THE BEATLES

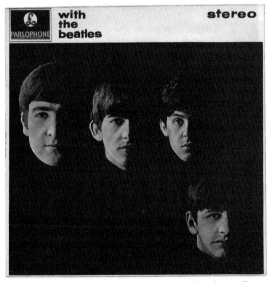

❏ Parlophone PMC 1206, mono, label has "Parlophone" standing alone in yellow, without "Sold in U.K. subject to resale price conditions, see price lists" underneath; "Recording first published 1963" at left , perimeter print begins with the words "THE PARLOPHONE CO. LTD.," with the publisher of "Money" listed as "Jobete," 1963 (ILLUS.) .... **60.00 - 120.00**

❑ Parlophone PMC 1206, mono, same as above, with the publisher of "Money" listed
as "Dominion, Belinda," 1963 .... **50.00 - 100.00**

❑ Parlophone PCS 3045, stereo, label has "Parlophone" standing alone in yellow,
without "Sold in U.K. subject to resale price conditions, see price lists" underneath;
"Recording first published 1963" at left , perimeter print begins with the words
"THE PARLOPHONE CO. LTD.," with the publisher of "Money" listed as "Jobete,"
1963 .... **125.00 - 250.00**

❑ Parlophone PCS 3045, stereo, same as above, with the publisher of "Money" listed
as "Dominion, Belinda," 1963 .... **100.00 - 200.00**

YELLOW SUBMARINE

(The front cover is basically the same as the U.S. version, but the back cover
is different.)

❑ Apple PMC 7070, mono; with "Sold in U.K. subject to resale price conditions, see
price lists" on label; back cover has red lines above and below the liner notes,
1969 .... **300.00 - 600.00**

❑ Apple PCS 7070, stereo; with "Sold in U.K. subject to resale price conditions, see
price lists" on label; back cover has red lines above and below the liner notes,
1969 .... **75.00 - 150.00**

LABEL VARIATIONS

After the condition of the record, the next most important element in determining the value of your Beatles records is its age. All editions of the same Beatles record are NOT created equal!

Curiously, for singles, the first pressings are often not the most valuable. In fact, because most copies of Beatles 45s were sold within the first several months to a year of release, original editions are often the most common version of a record. Because of the demand for top-notch originals, though, prices are solid despite their availability.

The rarest and most sought-after versions of Beatles singles are the short-lived "target" label design of 1969, with the Capitol "dome" logo at 9 o'clock. No original release of a Beatles 45 in the United States used this label, but it is by far the hardest to find if you are trying to collect every U.S. variation of a Beatles single.

> **TIP:** Almost every basic label has variations of type and layout, depending on where the label was printed. In most cases, these variations play no role in the value of the records.

45 RPM LABELS

Orange and yellow swirl without "A Subsidiary Of"... in perimeter label print: This is the original label for every Capitol single from "I Want to Hold Your Hand" through "Lady Madonna." It was used until the middle of 1968.

Orange and yellow swirl label with "A Subsidiary Of" in perimeter print in white: Used from the middle of 1968 to the middle of 1969, no original Beatles singles exist on this label.

Orange and yellow swirl label with "A Subsidiary Of" in perimeter print in black: Used briefly in 1969, this came only from East Coast pressing plants and is quite rare.

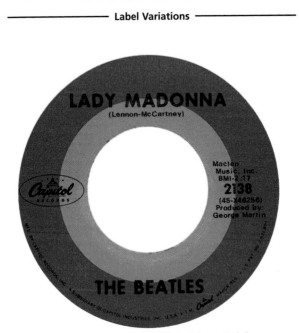

Red and orange "target" label with Capitol dome logo: This short-lived label was used for about four months in 1969. All Beatles 45s on this label are reissues, and all are rare.

Red and orange "target" label with Capitol round logo: Used from late 1969 to the spring of 1971 on Beatles 45s, no original Beatles 45s were on this label. Two slightly different versions exist; one has no white "dot" in the middle of rhe round logo, and the other one does.

Apple label with small Capitol logo on bottom of B-side label: Used from 1968 to 1970, this label appears on some, but not all, copies of all Apple 45s from "Hey Jude" through "The Long and Winding Road." These tend to be scarcer and thus more valuable than other Apple original 45 editions. No reissued Capitol title uses this label.

Apple label with "Mfd. by Apple" on label and no star: Used from 1968 to 1970 on many original copies of Apple 45s from "Hey Jude" to "The Long and Winding Road," plus on all reissues of Capitol 45s from the spring of 1971 to the end of 1974.

Apple label with star on A-side label: Only used in the spring and summer of 1971 on reissues of the Capitol singles, this is another sought-after variation.

Apple label with "All Rights Reserved" disclaimer:
Used on Beatles reissue singles in 1975 only. The disclaimer
can appear in any of several locations on the label. No
original Beatles 45 exists on this label.

Orange label with "Capitol" at bottom: Used from January 1976 to the middle of 1978. Almost every Capitol Beatles 45 is known to exist on this label. It also was the original issue label for the singles of "Got to Get You Into My Life" and "Ob-La-Di, Ob-La-Da."

Purple label (I): Used on Beatles reissue singles in the 5000s from mid-1978 to mid-1981 and in the 2000s well into the 1980s. They can be distinguished from the later purple label by a smaller label (to leave room for the 360 "notches" that usually appear along the label's edge) and the use of the abbreviation "Mfd." to start the perimeter print. This also is the original label for the single "Sgt. Pepper's Lonely Hearts Club Band/With a Little Help from My Friends."

Blue label: This appears on Beatles Capitol Starline reissues from 1981 to approximately 1985. All of the records in the 5000s were reassigned numbers in the 6200s and given these labels. No records in the 2000s use this label.

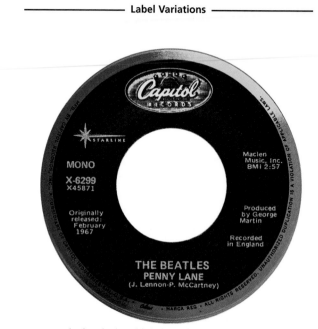

Black colorband label: Used on records in both the 6200s and 2000s from the mid-1980s to 1988. Also, this is the original label for the Capitol release of "Twist and Shout" (B-5624).

Purple label (II): Used on record in both the 6200s and 2000s from 1988 to 1990. It also was used on the various "For Jukeboxes Only!" singles from 1992 to 1996. They can be distinguished from the earlier purple label by a wider label (as Capitol no longer was using the 360 "notches" along the label's edge) and the use of the word "Manufactured" to start the perimeter print.

Album Labels

**Black colorband label without "A Subsidiary Of"...
in perimeter label print:** This is the original label for every
Capitol LP from Meet the Beatles! through Magical Mystery
Tour. All 1960s Beatles Capitol albums in mono use this label.

Black colorband label; border print adds "A Subsidiary of Capitol Industries Inc.": Used on reissues of Capitol LPs from mid-1968 to the end of 1969. Though all of these are scarcer than the originals, they are less valuable.

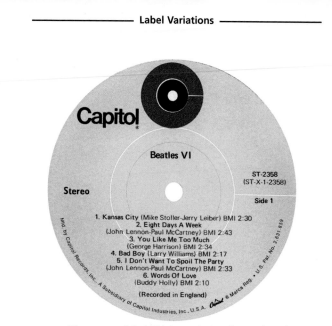

Lime green label: Used on reissues of Capitol LPs from the end of 1969 to the spring of 1971.

Red label with "target" Capitol at top: This label, similar in design to the lime green label, was used for Capitol LPs in the latter part of 1971 and the early part of 1972. The only Beatles album known to exist with this label is a reissue of Revolver, and it is quite valuable.

Apple label with Capitol logo on Side 2 bottom: Used from 1968 to 1971, this label appears on some, but not all, copies of all Apple LPs from The Beatles through Hey Jude. It was also used on Capitol albums reissued on Apple in 1971. These tend to be scarcer and thus more valuable than other Apple LP editions.

Apple label with "Mfd. by Apple" on label: Used from 1968 to 1970 on original Beatles albums and from 1971 to early 1975 on reissued Capitol Beatles LPs. A version of this label without the "Mfd. by Apple" was used for the Anthology vinyl editions.

Apple label with "All Rights Reserved" disclaimer:
Used on Beatles reissue LPs in 1975 only. The disclaimer can
appear in any of several locations on the label.

Orange label with "All Rights Reserved" on label:
Used on Beatles reissue LPs from early 1976 to mid-1978.
Newly released Beatles LPs in this period had custom labels.

Purple label, large Capitol logo on top: Used for Beatles reissue LPs from mid-1978 to early 1983. This is easily distinguishable from the later purple label because of the huge size of the Capitol logo at the top and two separate sections of perimeter print. Newly released Beatles LPs in this period had custom labels.

Black label, print in colorband: Appears on Beatles reissue LPs from early 1983 to 1987. Also used on the original editions of the 1980 Rarities LP as a custom label, and on the first U.S. releases of the British versions of the original albums (Please Please Me, With the Beatles, A Hard Day's Night, Beatles for Sale, Help!, Rubber Soul and Revolver).

Purple label, small Capitol logo at top: Used on Beatles reissue LPs from 1988 to 1990. This is easily distinguishable from the earlier purple label because of the small size of the Capitol logo at the top and the one continuous line of perimeter print.

Ex-Beatlemania

By Casey Piotrowski

It was an amazing time. The Beatles were constantly at the top of the charts. Seemingly, every time you turned on the radio, you heard a new Beatles record. They were always in the press or on TV. Who can forget those incredible days of 1974? That's right, 1974…really mid-1973 through mid-1975.

Because of the way they controlled pop music as a group in 1964, almost overlooked was the way they nearly duplicated (and in some ways surpassed) the feat as solo artists a decade later.

Certainly, immediately after the breakup, the Beatles' enormous popularity gave momentum to the fledgling solo careers of John, Paul, George and Ringo. In fact, each had a No. 1 single million-seller within 18 months of the group's breakup. But, by 1972, much of that early goodwill had dried up.

John Lennon was coming off his *Some Time In New York City* disaster, an album that peaked no higher than No. 33 nationally, along with the even-then politically incorrectly titled single "Woman Is The Nigger Of The World," which peaked no higher than No. 57 nationally (in *Billboard*) and couldn't break the top 85 in either Cashbox or Record World.

Paul McCartney was ravaged by the press for his first Wings LP, *Wildlife,* which peaked at No. 8 (after his first two LPs each topped the charts). And neither of his first two Wings singles could crack the American Top 20. The first, "Give Ireland Back To The Irish," was panned for being too political. The second, "Mary Had A Little Lamb," was knocked

for not being political enough. George Harrison had gone two and a half years since his last studio album and 18 months since his last single, and that ("Bangla Desh") failed to make the national Top 15. And Ringo Starr had only two pop singles (though both Top 10 hits) and two specialized albums, neither of which had Beatles-esque chart numbers (the album of standards, *Sentimental Journey,* peaked at No. 20 and the country album, *Beaucoups of Blues,* peaked at No. 31) in the more than three years since the group broke up.

Fans of the group had to wonder just how much each needed the others professionally, if not personally.

A modest return to form began with McCartney's "Hi, Hi, Hi" single, which peaked at No. 6 in Cashbox in February 1973. But the comeback began in earnest, ironically enough, with the first post-breakup releases from the group, the '62-'66 and the '67-'70 greatest hits packages. Each hit No. 1, though, oddly enough, not in the same national publications ('67-'70 reached No. 1 in Billboard, '62-'66 in both Cashbox and Record World). This was in late May 1973, but before either album could get comfortable in the top spot, it had competition from within the family. That started a run on the charts that had only been seen once before.

In late May, '67-'70 was knocked out of the top spot by McCartney's Red Rose Speedway, which was, in turn, knocked out of the top spot by Harrison's Living In The Material World. Continuously, from mid-May to the end of July, a Beatles album, either from one of the group or the group as a whole, was in No. 1. It was something that hadn't been seen since it was done 10 years earlier by, guess who? And, in an achievement that rivaled their having the nation's top five singles in April 1964, these four albums were all in the top five of Cashbox's album chart for the week ending June 23, 1973. This was something that never happened even during the halcyon days of 1964.

Meanwhile, McCartney's ballad from Speedway, "My Love," was racing up the singles chart, hitting the No. 1 spot on June 2 (becoming, surprisingly, the first time a Beatle had hit the top spot in more than 18 months). It stayed there for four months, until McCartney was again knocked out of No. 1 by Harrison with his "Give Me Love" single.

By the time Harrison was falling from the Top 10, he was replaced by McCartney with his "Live And Let Die" single, which would also hit No. 1 (in Cashbox and Record World). When the James Bond theme finally left the Top 10 near the end of September, it ended a string of four months when at least one Beatle had a single in the Top 10. And before "Live And Let Die" dropped off the chart completely, the other ex-members of the group were about to be heard from.

Starr was then climbing the charts with "Photograph." As it reached the Top 10 (in Billboard on Nov. 10, 1973), Lennon was climbing the charts with his "Mind Games" single, which would hit the Top 10 in both Cashbox and Record World. By the time "Photograph" reached No. 1 (Nov. 23, 1973), McCartney was back on the charts with "Helen Wheels." Within three weeks, the Beatles would have three records in the Top 20. In fact, with the exception of two weeks, from Oct. 27, 1973, to June 29, 1974, more than eight months, there was always at least one record from some member of the group in the Top 10, something that the group never achieved while together. During that time, besides "Photograph," "Band On The Run" and "You're Sixteen" both hit No. 1. "Oh My My," "Jet" and "Helen Wheels" all hit the Top 5 nationally.

The action on the album charts was no different. The Ringo album was in the Top 10 by its third week on the charts (Nov. 23, 1973) and was joined there by Lennon's Mind Games LP, followed closely by McCartney's Band On The Run album. By the first week of January 1974, all three solo albums were in the national Top 20. Never before (or since)

had three solo projects from members of the same group charted that high simultaneously. Both Ringo and Band On The Run would peak at No. 1. Mind Games would top out at No. 6. The charts had a chance to cool down a bit. (There were no singles on the charts from any of the four from Aug. 24, 1974 to Sept. 21, 1974). But it was only the calm before the storm.

Lennon was first out of the box with "Whatever Gets You Through The Night," which debuted on the charts on Sept. 28, 1974. It would reach No. 1 eight weeks later, as McCartney's single, "Junior's Farm," and Starr's first release from Goodnight Vienna, "Only You," and Harrison's "Dark Horse" were also on the way to becoming major hits. On Nov. 30, 1974, all of the Beatles would have a single in the Top 40. In fact, from mid-November 1974 to mid-February 1975, a period of 13 weeks, each of the Beatles had at least one single continuously on the charts at the same time. And, during one week (Jan. 25, 1975), the four of them collectively had seven of the Top 10 singles in the country, a feat not matched since…well, you know.

It was no different on the album charts. While Band On The Run was concluding its phenomenal run on the charts, Lennon's Walls and Bridges was headed for No. 1, which it would reach on Nov. 16, 1974. Two weeks after Lennon's album fell from the Top 10 (Dec. 21), Starr's Goodnight

Vienna LP took its place, eventually peaking at No. 5 (in Record World). Harrison's Dark Horse album, which would climb as high as No. 4, would join it in the Top 10 for the last two weeks of January 1975, the last time two members of the same band would have Top 10 albums at the same time. Within two weeks of Dark Horse dropping from the Top 20 (Feb. 22, 1975), Lennon's Rock 'N' Roll climbed to that level on the charts on its way to No. 4 (in Record World). During the period from Dec. 21, 1974, to April 19, 1975, all four members of the group had albums continuously on the chart.

As Lennon's album left the Top 10 at the end of April, this incredible run by the Beatles, separately this time, would end. Lennon would give us nothing new for more than five years until his tragically brief comeback. Harrison's "This Guitar" single, released in December 1975, would fail to chart in any of the national trades. Starr would never see the sunny side of the Top 20, either album or single, charts again. Even McCartney, who would have three more No. 1 albums in a row, couldn't get his "Letting Go" single any higher than No. 39 in October 1975.

But there's no taking away from what the four of them had achieved during the previous 24 months. Each member of the group had at least one No. 1 single and one No. 1 album...seven No. 1 albums in all. Eight No. 1 singles in two years. Five gold singles. Eleven gold albums (again, something they couldn't match in their years together). Four more singles hitting the Top 5. Three more hitting the Top 10. Collectively, 35 weeks in the singles Top 10 in 1973, 33 weeks in 1974, 48 weeks in the album Top 10 in 1973 (with the first album not getting there until the end of April) and 42 weeks there in 1974.

All this came during a time when radio station formats were getting fragmented and playlists getting smaller. Also, unlike 1964, each of those releases gave competition, not synergy, to the others. Each solo release would be looked upon as a new "Beatles" record, and stations would hesitate adding, for example, a new Lennon record if they were already playing something from McCartney, Harrison or Starr.

It was a tribute not only to immense popularity of these four men, but also to their immense talent. No one

can make this kind of a sustained chart run on personality alone. Looking back, much of the music that these four men produced individually during that time still ranks with the most creative and entertaining work of the era, as was the case of their work as a group 10 years before.

Just as no group has since dominated the charts as John, Paul, George and Ringo did in 1964, no group of individuals has since dominated the charts as John, Paul, George and Ringo did 10 years later.

Conspicuous By Their Absence

By Casey Piotrowski

The Beatles' predominance in American rock 'n' roll in the 1960s? Oh, yeah, I heard something about that. The 23 No. 1 singles? Not bad. The 16 No. 1 albums? Worth a mention. Had all of the Top 5 singles in America in April 1964. Probably beginner's luck.

Obviously, what the Beatles did during those magnificent seven years before their breakup was remarkable. But don't forget, during all that time, the Beatles were there, selling their music as well as making it. They toured, made movies, had TV and radio appearances and, eventually, produced music videos. Seemingly, they always had time for an interview or a photo op. (Try finding a music magazine from that time that didn't feature a piece on the Beatles.) There was always a steady stream of great new product being released.

But how their success as a group continued after their breakup may be an even greater achievement. Remember, after 1970, all "new" Beatles product consisted of repackages (Beatles fans who bought Reel Music enjoyed the privilege of getting "And I Love Her" for the seventh time) or the group's own second choices.

Frequently, those packages would have to compete with usually good, often great, new solo releases from the group's members. Instead of John, Paul, George and Ringo celebrating their past, the four of them have spent the best part of the last 30 years throwing rocks at the group's legacy and at each other. That's hardly the best way to promote your

catalog. Still, the public knew much better. It is the fans' loyalty and the quality of the group's work that has made the Beatles the most successful music act not only from 1964 to 1970, but, arguably, from 1970 to today as well. Without question, they have enjoyed more success after their breakup than any other act.

Consider the following: Since the invention of the longplay record, only 11 acts (besides the Beatles) have had as many as five No. 1 albums. The Beatles have had that

many No. 1 albums since they broke up ('62-'66, '67-'70 and all three volumes of Anthology). Along with that, three other Beatles packages (Hollywood Bowl, Live At The BBC and Rock 'N' Roll Music) peaked at No. 2. Using that as the yardstick, over the last 30 years, only Paul McCartney (in all permutations of his solo career), with 10, and The Rolling Stones, with nine, have charted more albums as high as the disbanded Beatles. (And we're not counting two more No. 1 albums—Let It Be, new recordings released after the group's

breakup, and The Beatles Again [Hey Jude], which held No. 2 the week the group split.) In fact, discounting the new reunion recordings from the Eagles and Fleetwood Mac, no band has had even one archival release hit No. 1—much less five of them. If we stretch that point to include solo artists, only two of them have had albums reach No. 1 after their deaths—Janis Joplin (Pearl) and, predictably enough, John Lennon (Double Fantasy).

In their native England, it was more of the same. Both Hollywood Bowl and Live At The BBC hit No. 1, as did the five other titles that reached No. 1 in America, giving the Beatles seven No. 1 albums in their homeland after their split. (Three more albums, Love Songs, 20 Greatest Hits and Rock 'N' Roll Music, also hit the Top 10.) In the past three decades, only four other artists (McCartney, Queen, ABBA and David Bowie) hit No. 1 more frequently than the Beatles did after they broke up!

A couple more quick notes about their post-breakup albums. The Beatles hit No. 1 three times in one year with the release of Anthology 1, 2 and 3. Only Elvis Presley, who did it in 1960, and the Beatles themselves, who had four No. 1 albums in 1964 and three No. 1s in 1965, 1966 and 1970, hit the top spot on the album chart that many times in one year. (They would have done it in 1969, too, but Yellow Submarine was blocked from No. 1 by Abbey Road.) No other band has had three albums debut at No. 1 (which all three volumes of Anthology did).

As for singles, the Beatles have had four major hit singles since their breakup. (We're not counting "The Long And Winding Road," which was already in pre-release when McCartney announced his intention to leave the group.) In order of their release, they include "Got To Get You Into My Life," which peaked at No. 3, "The Beatles Movie Medley" (No. 12), "Free As A Bird" (No. 6), and "Real Love (No. 10). No other band has hit the Top 10 even once after their breakup.

Even reunion efforts from other bands failed to do much. The Eagles' terrific "Get Over It" could do no better than No. 15. Fleetwood Mac, with a tour and a No. 1 album to support them, couldn't chart either of the wonderful singles from The Dance ("Silver Springs" and "Landslide").

Only three solo artists had major hits after their passing: Janis Joplin ("Me And Bobby McGee," hitting No. 1), Jim Croce ("Time In A Bottle" hitting No. 10 and "I'll Have To Say I Love You In A Song" peaking at No. 12) and, of course, John Lennon ("Woman" hitting No. 1, "Nobody Told Me" hitting No. 5 and "Watching The Wheels" hitting No. 10). But the chart success of those artists pretty much stopped not long after their deaths. The Beatles have had at least one major hit in every decade since their breakup.

(In Britain, "Movie Medley" hit the Top 10. So did "Yesterday," finally released as a single there in 1976. "Love Me Do" finally became a Top 5 there with its 20th anniversary release in 1982. "Baby It's You" from Live At The BBC hit No. 7 in 1993. Both "Free As A Bird" and "Real Love" hit the Top 5 in 1996. That gave the Beatles six Top 10 singles in the U.K. after their split.)

As for gold singles, the recent certification of "Got To Get You Into My Life" gave the Beatles three singles released after their breakup to go gold. No other disbanded group has even one. As for departed solo artists, Elvis Presley (with "Way Down" and "My Way") has two. Lennon, Joplin and Croce have one each.

Speaking of 24-carat hardware, while together the Beatles earned 19 gold albums. They've earned 20 more gold albums with packages released after their breakup. In fact, every package Capitol has issued since the group's split has gone at least gold; most have gone platinum. The '62-'66 and '67-'70 packages have earned the RIAA's new diamond

certification with sales of more than 10 million units each. Rock 'N' Roll Music has gone gold three different ways—as a double album and as two single albums.

In the past 30 years, as record sales have exploded, more than 20 artists have earned at least 21 gold albums. It's a list wide enough to include The Rolling Stones, Elton John, Barbra Streisand, George Strait and Kiss.

Still, for the Beatles—who spent much of the last three decades not speaking to each other, much less working together—to average one gold album every 15 months for 30 years after they've broken up is staggering.

All in all, they haven't done badly. While the artists who followed in the '70s, '80s and '90s worked intently to perfect their art and then feverishly to sell it, the Beatles just about matched them stride for stride while pretty much doing nothing.

The part of the Beatles' history—where they threw away their crowns but remained kings nonetheless—is overlooked. Though it doesn't contribute to the body of their work, it does add to the legacy of their popularity. It offers more proof that the Beatles didn't just fill our ears, they also filled our hearts.

Together When We're Apart

By Casey Piotrowski

Certainly, it is the most unforgettable breakup in the history of rock 'n' roll. With the possible exception of the split between Dean Martin and Jerry Lewis, no breakup in the history of show business has received as much attention.

April 10, 1970—It's a day that will live in rock infamy, an event so big that each of the principals felt the need to address it in his work (John Lennon's "How Do You Sleep," Paul McCartney's "Dear Friend," George Harrison's "Sue Me, Sue You Blues" and Ringo Starr's "Early 1970," among a number of other titles). It is an event so large in rock's history that it merits being written about, as this article demonstrates, more than 30 years after the fact.

The dream was over. The Beatles had broken up.

Or had they? After Martin and Lewis split, they never appeared in each other's movies or TV shows or on each other's records. The Police have been apart for years, yet Sting, Andy Summers and Stewart Copeland have given each other precious little help in their respective solo efforts. The Eagles, the preeminent band of the 1970s, each enjoyed some degree of solo success before their mid-'90s reunion, but almost none of it came with the assistance of their fellow bandmates.

Fleetwood Mac is another band where its members (most notably Stevie Nicks, Lindsay Buckingham and Christine

McVie) would move in and out of the band, record as solo artists and do quite well for themselves. But each did it largely on their own, without contributions from the band they were ultimately still a part of.

But the Beatles had broken up, and their split was bitter, vicious. They dragged each other through the mud in the courts, in the press, even on their own solo records. (According to their partnership, McCartney shared equally with Lennon in the profits of Lennon's *Imagine* LP—even as McCartney was continually skewered musically by his former partner.)

The Beatles with producer George Martin.

The Beatles didn't just break up the band. They took sledgehammers to it, ran over it with a tank, then threw it into an atom smasher just for good measure. If members of any band had reason to go their separate ways and never, absolutely never look back, it was the Beatles.

Of course, that never happened.

The last three-plus decades are filled with examples of the Beatles in twos, threes and yes, sometimes even all four of them, working with each other and with George Martin. We include Martin here because he was more than just their producer, their arranger or the igniter of their imaginations. More than any other person, Martin has earned the right to be called their collaborator. He has been the architect of their sound, their growth, their creative legend. He has been the fifth side of the square. And any look at the collaborations of the ex-Beatles has to include their work with him.

But, getting back to that breakup. If the Beatles really hated each other so much, why did Lennon plug McCartney's "Coming Up" when he was in the midst of his own comeback? Why did Harrison help Starr write "It Don't Come Easy" yet not accept co-writer's credit? Why did Harrison agree to play a slide guitar solo on McCartney's "Wanderlust"? Why indeed.

Perhaps each of the Beatles were using professional reasons to express their personal feelings, practicing while apart what they so consistently preached while they were together—love, in this case, for one another.

Maybe it was like Harrison said in "When We Was Fab"—"The microscopes that magnified the tears." As vicious as it may have seemed at the time, perhaps the worst of their split really lasted only a few embarrassingly public moments. With the perspective of time, it's clear that the rift among the four was nowhere as deep as it appeared. Time has also showed us that as much as each needed to go out and prove his own mettle, each still ultimately realized that he needed the other three around.

With that in mind, we thought it would be interesting to see, in light of all the acrimony—real and imagined—just

how frequently these four guys wound up working together after that fateful day in April more than three decades ago.

We turned to three marvelously well-researched books—*Eight Arms To Hold You* by Chip Madinger and Mark Easter, *Beatles Undercover* by Kristofer Engelhardt and *The Beatles After The Break-Up* by Keith Badman—as primary reference sources and put together a fairly complete list of John, Paul, George and Ringo's work together after the Beatles.

We think you'll be surprised and, if you're a Beatles fan, quite pleasantly so, as we look at the post-separation work of a band that never quite broke up.

First, we'll look at their work together—long before their split.

1960

Ringo (at that time still the drummer for Rory Storm & The Hurricanes) joins John, Paul and George in the studio to play on Lu Walters' recording of "Summertime." (Oct. 15, 1960)

1963

All four Beatles play on a (recently discovered) demo for "I'll Be On My Way," intended for Billy J. Kramer & The Dakotas.

1964

Lennon and McCartney do the arrangement, McCartney plays piano and Martin produces "It's For You," a song McCartney wrote for Cilla Black (July 2, 1964)

1965

Lennon and Harrison do background vocals on a broadcast version of Adam Faith's "I Need Your Lovin'." (April 16, 1965)

Lennon produces, McCartney plays guitar and Harrison plays tambourine on The Silkie's version of "You've Got To Hide Your Love Away." (Aug. 9, 1965)

1966

McCartney writes the soundtrack for *The Family Way*. Martin produces. (Sept. 10, 1966)

1967

Lennon and McCartney add backing vocals to The Rolling Stones' "We Love You." (May 18, 1967)

Lennon and Harrison appear on British TV's *David Frost Show*. (Oct. 4, 1967)

1968

Lennon and McCartney help produce The Grapefruit's single "Dear Delilah." (Jan. 19, 1968)

Martin produces McCartney's "Step Inside Love" for Cilla Black. (Feb. 28, 1968)

Lennon and McCartney appear on *The Tonight Show*. (May 15, 1968)

Harrison and Starr are interviewed for the BBC television documentary *All My Loving*. (May 23, 1968)

Harrison produces, plays and writes, and McCartney and Starr play on Jackie Lomax's *Is This What You Want?* LP. (June 24, 1968)

McCartney produces, Martin plays piano on Mary Hopkin's *Postcard* LP.

McCartney writes the liner notes for Lennon and Yoko Ono's *Two Virgins* LP.

McCartney plays bass and Harrison sings background vocals on James Taylor's "Carolina On My Mind."

1969

Lennon, McCartney and Starr appear playing an untitled jam in Yoko's film *Then & Now.* (Jan. 10, 1969; film released December 1984)

All four Beatles back up Billy Preston as he records demos for two of his own songs. (Jan. 28, 1969)

Lennon and McCartney play on Ono's "Lennon, Lennon (Let's Hope For Peace)." (Jan. 23, 1969, version was not released)

Harrison plays and Martin produces an early version of "It Don't Come Easy." (This version was not released)

McCartney produces and Harrison plays on Jackie Lomax's "Thumbin' A Ride" and "Going Back To Liverpool." (March 1969)

Starr appears on Martin's YTV special *With A Little Help From My Friends*. (Aug. 14, 1969)

McCartney and Starr play on "Qué Será, Será" and "The Fields of St. Etienne." (August 1969)

Starr plays on Lennon's "Cold Turkey." (Sept. 25, 1969)

Harrison and Starr play on Leon Russell's self-titled LP. (September 1969)

Harrison plays with Lennon's Plastic Ono Band (and a cast of thousands) at the Benefit For UNICEF. (Dec. 15, 1969)

Lennon makes a cameo appearance and McCartney contributes "Come & Get It" for Starr's film *The Magic Christian*.

McCartney arranges "Stardust" for Starr's *Sentimental Journey* LP.

Martin produces Starr's *Sentimental Journey* LP. (Sessions continued into 1970)

Harrison produces, writes and plays, and Starr plays on Doris Troy's self-titled LP. (Sessions continued into 1970)

1970

Harrison plays lead guitar on Lennon's "Instant Karma." (Jan. 28, 1970)

Harrison produces and plays lead guitar on Starr's "It Don't Come Easy." (March 1970)

Harrison produces, writes and plays, and Starr plays on Preston's *Encouraging Words* LP. (April 6 1970)

Lennon produces and plays, and Starr plays on Ono's *Plastic Ono Band* LP. (Sept. 10, 1970)

Harrison plays lead guitar on Starr's "Early 1970." (October 1970)

Lennon, Harrison and Starr play on Ono's "Greenfield Morning, I Pushed An Empty Baby Carriage All Over The City." (October 1970)

Starr plays on Lennon's *Plastic Ono Band* LP. (Oct. 11, 1970)

Starr plays on Harrison's *All Things Must Pass* LP. (May 10, 1970)

According to drummer Alan White, Lennon plays on Harrison's "My Sweet Lord."

Harrison and Starr play on "In Praise Of Lord," an unreleased track by Aashish Khan.

Lennon, McCartney, Harrison and Starr appear on BBC Radio One's special *Let It Be*.

1971

Lennon contributes background vocals to Ronnie Spector's "Tandoori Chicken," which Harrison produced. (Feb. 1, 1971)

Lennon produces and Starr plays on the Elastic Oz Band's "God Save Oz," which Lennon wrote. A version with Lennon's lead vocal is subsequently released on *The John Lennon Anthology*. (May 1, 1971)

Harrison plays on Lennon's *Imagine* LP. (May 1971)

Harrison and Starr play at The Concert For Bangla Desh. (Aug. 1, 1971)

Martin arranges orchestration for the New York Philharmonic on McCartney's "Uncle Albert/Admiral Halsey."

Harrison and Starr play on an unreleased recording by British actor Nicol Williamson.

All four Beatles and Martin give new interviews for the BBC radio series *The Beatles Story*. (The series is broadcast from May to August 1972)

1972

Harrison and Starr play on Harry Nilsson's *Son of Schmilsson* LP. (March 3, 1972)

Harrison produces and writes, and Starr plays on "You've Got To Stay With Me" and "I'll Still Love You" for Black. (August 1972)

Harrison and Starr play on Nilsson's "Daybreak" single. (September 1972)

Martin produces McCartney's "Live & Let Die." (October 1972)

Starr plays on Harrison's *Living In The Material World* LP. (Oct. 10-11, 1972)

Harrison produces and plays lead guitar on Starr's "Back Off Boogaloo." (Starr later admits that, though uncredited, Harrison helped him write the song.)

1973

Lennon, McCartney and Harrison write, sing and play on the *Starr* LP. (March 4, 1973)

Harrison produces and plays, and Starr plays on the *Shankar Family & Friends* LP. (April 1973)

Starr plays on Harrison's "Ding Dong, Ding Dong" single. (November 1973)

1974

Lennon produces, writes and sings, and Starr drums on Nilsson's *Pussy Cats* LP. (April 6, 1974)

Lennon writes, plays and sings on Starr's *Goodnight Vienna* LP. Versions of Lennon singing lead on "Only You" and "Goodnight Vienna" are subsequently released on *The John Lennon Anthology*. (Aug. 11, 1974)

Lennon does the voice-over for TV and radio commercials for Starr's *Goodnight Vienna*. (Nov. 14, 1974)

Starr does the voice-over for TV and radio commercials for Lennon's *Walls & Bridges*. (Nov. 14, 1974)

Lennon and Harrison appear (though not together) from Harrison's hotel room in a radio interview following Harrison's last stop on his 1974 American tour. (Dec. 20, 1974)

1975

Martin is interviewed for the ABC TV special *David Frost Salutes The Beatles*. (May 21, 1974)

1976

Lennon and McCartney write and play, and Harrison writes for Starr's *Rotogravure* LP. (April 6, 1976)

Starr joins McCartney on stage during his L.A. Forum concert appearance. Their backstage meeting appears on McCartney's *Wings Over The World* TV special, which aired in 1979. (June 21, 1976)

Martin remixes tracks for the Beatles' *Rock & Roll Music* repackage.

1977

All four Beatles give their consent to the release of *The Beatles At The Hollywood Bowl*.

McCartney and Martin are interviewed for the Beatles' episode of ITV's *All You Need Is Love* series.

1978

Harrison appears on the Starr TV special.

Harrison and Martin are interviewed for a Capitol Radio feature on the Beatles.

Lennon records several demos for Starr's (then-titled) *Can't Fight Lightning* LP (later to be called *Stop And Smell The Roses*).

1980

McCartney appears on the episode of *This Is Your Life* honoring Martin. (Jan. 30, 1980)

McCartney writes, plays and sings on Starr's *Can't Fight Lightning* LP. (July 1980)

Martin begins sitting through McCartney's demos to choose material for the next Wings LP, which will become McCartney's solo *Tug of War*. (August 1980)

Harrison produces, writes, sings and plays on Starr's *Can't Fight Lightning/Stop And Smell The Roses* LP. (Nov. 19-25, 1980)

Martin produces McCartney's *Tug of War* LP.

(Lennon is killed by gunfire in New York City on Dec. 8, 1980.)

1981

Starr drums on Harrison's *Somewhere In England* LP. (February 1981)

Starr drums for McCartney's *Tug of War*. (Feb. 15-19, 1981)

Starr and Martin appear in a video for McCartney's "Take It Away." (June 18-23, 1981)

McCartney sings, Starr plays and Martin assists in the production of Harrison's "All Those Years Ago."

McCartney produces and appears with Starr in *The Cooler*, an 11-minute video featuring music from Starr's *Stop And Smell The Roses*.

1982

Martin presents a check to the recipient of the first John Lennon Scholarship. (Nov. 13, 1982)

Martin produces tracks for McCartney's *Pipes of Peace*. Starr plays on McCartney's "Average Person."

Martin does interviews for United Artists' *The Compleat Beatles* video.

1983

Starr costars in McCartney's film *Give My Regards To Broad Street*. (Feb. 5, 1983)

Starr plays and Martin produces McCartney's *Give My Regards To Broad Street*.

McCartney and Martin are taped for LWT's *South Bank Show*. (Nov. 12, 1983)

McCartney and Martin appear on the BBC TV program *Hardy*. (Dec. 14, 1983)

1984

Martin collects McCartney's Ivor Novello Award for "We All Stand Together." (March 13, 1984)

Starr appears in McCartney's *So Sad* video.

Harrison and Starr appear (playing in a concert segment) in the film *Water* (which was released by Harrison's Handmade Films).

Harrison writes and plays, and Starr plays on the soundtrack of *Water*.

1985

Harrison and Starr play and sing on the Carl Perkins' *Blue Suede Shoes* special. (Oct. 21, 1985)

1986

McCartney and Starr contribute tracks to *The Anti-Heroin Project: It's A Live-In World* benefit LP. (released Nov. 24, 1986)

Martin begins remixes of the Beatles recordings for release on CD.

1987

Starr plays drums on Harrison's *Cloud Nine* LP. (Jan. 8, 1987)

McCartney and Harrison play (separately) on Duane Eddy's self-titled LP. (February 1987)

Harrison and Starr appear at the Prince's Trust Benefit Concert at Wembley Arena. (June 5-8, 1987)

Martin orchestrates and mixes McCartney's "Once Upon A Long Ago" and produces overdubs on two other McCartney songs. (July 1, 1987)

Martin produces McCartney's music for his *Rupert The Bear* animated film. (Dec. 1, 1987)

Harrison and Starr shoot a video for Harrison's "When We Was Fab" video. (Dec. 18, 1987)

Martin produces the soundtrack for McCartney's unreleased animated film *Tropical Island Hum*.

1988

Harrison and Starr attend the Beatles' induction into The Rock And Roll Hall Of Fame. (Jan. 20, 1988)

Harrison and Starr appear together on TV's *Aspel & Company* talk show. (March 3, 1988)

Martin does the string arrangements for McCartney's "Put It There."

Martin prepares Beatles music for use in the *John Lennon: Imagine* movie.

1989

McCartney and Martin appear on French TV's *Sacree Soiree*. (May 31, 1989)

1990

Starr records "I Call Your Name" to be used for the John Lennon Scholarship Concert. (March 1990)

McCartney's taped performance is played at the John Lennon Scholarship Concert in Liverpool.

McCartney is interviewed for BBC Radio 1's series *In My Life: Lennon Remembered*. (broadcast Oct. 6, 1990)

Harrison and Starr contribute tracks to the *Nobody's Child—Romanian Angel Appeal* charity CD. All four Beatles wives co-chair the effort.

1991

McCartney writes and demos "Angels In Disguise" for Starr's *Time Takes Time* LP. The track was not released.

1992

Harrison and Starr play together at the Natural Law Party benefit concert. (April 6, 1992)

Martin produces McCartney's "Calico Skies" and "Great Day." The songs would not be released until McCartney's 1997 *Flaming Pie* LP.

McCartney, Harrison and Starr appear on Martin's ITV and Disney Channel special *The Making Of Sgt. Pepper*.

Martin arranges orchestral overdubs for McCartney's "C'mon People."

1993

Starr joins McCartney on stage at The Hollywood Bowl for the chorus of "Hey Jude." (April 16, 1993)

Harrison joins Martin for a press conference to launch the CD release of *The Beatles '62-'66* and *'67-'70*. (Sept. 9, 1993)

McCartney and Starr make separate guest appearances on the ITV special *Cilla—A Celebration*. (September 1993)

McCartney and Harrison tape interviews for MTV Europe's Beatle Day. (Nov. 1, 1993)

1994

McCartney inducts Lennon into The Rock And Roll Hall of Fame. (Jan. 19, 1994)

McCartney, Harrison and Starr begin their "reunion" sessions, which will ultimately yield "Free As A Bird." (Feb. 11, 1994)

Martin prepares *Beatles Live At The BBC*.

McCartney and Starr appear in the "Drive My Car" promotional message for Recording Artists, Actors And Athletes Against Drunk Driving.

1995

McCartney, Harrison and Starr complete "Real Love" from Lennon's demo. (Jan. 2, 1995)

1996

Starr sings and plays on McCartney's *Flaming Pie*. (May 1996)

All four Beatles contribute music to Perkins' *Go Cat Go* LP.

McCartney, Harrison and Starr do interviews to promote the *Anthology 3* CDs.

1997

Martin arranges the orchestra for McCartney's "Beautiful Night." (Feb. 14, 1997)

Starr and Martin are interviewed for McCartney's *Flaming Pie* radio special. (April 1997)

McCartney plays at the Music for Monserrat concert organized by Martin. Martin conducts the orchestra for McCartney's performance of the medley from *Abbey Road*. (Sept. 15, 1997)

Starr appears in McCartney's "Beautiful Night" video. (October 1997)

Starr and Martin contribute interviews for the Black episode of the Granada TV series *Brit Girls*.

McCartney tapes a segment for George Martin's *Rhythm of Life* TV series. (Dec. 28, 1997)

Starr and Harrison appear in McCartney's *In The World Tonight* documentary.

McCartney plays and sings, Harrison plays, and Martin arranges on Starr's *Vertical Man* LP.

1998

McCartney and Martin are interviewed for ITV's documentary *The Story Of Abbey Road*.

McCartney, Harrison and Starr all send video congratulations as Martin is presented with an Outstanding Achievement award at the Music Industry Trust's Dinner in London. (Oct. 23, 1998)

Martin appears on the Lennon episode of VH-1's *Legends* series. (Dec. 8, 1998)

Martin produces *The Lennon Anthology* version of Lennon's "Grow Old With Me."

1999

Martin conducts the Tribute To The Beatles concert to reopen The Hollywood Bowl. (June 25, 1999)

McCartney, Harrison and Starr all take a "strong interest" in and are interviewed for the re-release of the *Yellow Submarine* movie.

2000

McCartney, Harrison and Starr work on *The Beatles Anthology* DVD release.

McCartney, Harrison and Starr are interviewed for *The Beatles Anthology* book.

2001

Harrison and Starr perform (on separate tracks) for the Larry "Legs" Smith album.

Harrison and Starr perform (on separate tracks) for the new Electric Light Orchestra album *Zoom*.

McCartney does the introduction for Starr's All Starr Band DVD and TV special.

(Harrison dies on Nov. 29, 2001)

2002

McCartney and Starr join many of Harrison's friends at the Concert For George, later released on DVD. (Nov. 29, 2002)

All in all, it's pretty amazing. Every year since their breakup—more than three decades now—there's been at least one project, usually many more, in which two or more of the Beatles have participated. In the last several years, since their rapprochement, those projects have, again, centered around the group.

Knowing how loathe all four of them have been through the years to talk of a reunion, there's probably a good chance that there has been other work between two or three or even all four of them over the years that we'll never know about. But that is speculation.

This much is fact—the days of divisiveness among the Beatles are far outnumbered by the years of cooperation, support and love on both sides of the "breakup."

One of the most appealing qualities of the Beatles has been their willingness to support one another, whether it related directly to the band or not. We saw it when Harrison and Starr hawked Lennon's book, *In His Own Write,* on an early 1960s BBC radio appearance; when the other three stood by Lennon during the "bigger than Jesus" controversy; when they stood by McCartney after Linda's death; and when McCartney told fans to "boycott that book" after the release of Albert Goldman's scandalous *The Life And Times Of John Lennon,* and countless times in between. After 40-plus years, this kind of unity has become as much a part of the Beatles' persona as shaggy hair and "yeah, yeah, yeah."

Maybe the same can be said for members of all bands, but with the Beatles' level of fame and the individual recognition for each that has come with it, this particular example of male bonding seems unique.

For that kind of loyalty to exist for this long a time seems remarkable, particularly among men who have reached the station in life these four have. If anything, each has proven time and again that he doesn't need the other three to achieve either commercial or artistic success. Ultimately, they have chosen to remain in each other's lives.

In his last words on the Beatles, Derek Taylor called their story "the 20th century's greatest romance" and, as we work our way through the beginnings of a new millennium, that love story—between the Beatles and the world and among the Beatles themselves—goes on.

ACKNOWLEDGMENTS

This book would not have been possible without generous contributions from several of the United States' top experts on the Beatles and their records:

- Bruce Spizer of New Orleans, La. During the past few years, he painstakingly researched the Beatles' output on virtually every American label on which they appeared. Most of the photos in this book are from his work. If you want to see even more examples of Beatles covers and labels, and find out the stories behind them, I recommend his books, *The Beatles' Records on Vee-Jay* (now out of print), *The Beatles' Story on Capitol Records* (two volumes, one on singles, one on albums), *The Beatles on Apple Records, The Beatles Are Coming! The Birth of Beatlemania in America,* and *The Beatles Solo on Apple Records.* The available books can be found at his Web site (www.beatle.net).
- Gary Hein of Little Silver, N.J., a dealer in Beatles records and memorabilia since the 1970s. You can find out more about his offerings at his Web site (www.beatles4me.com).

■ Larry Marion and Marc Zakarin of
ItsOnlyRocknRoll.com, an auction house
in New York that specializes in rock-
music memorabilia. To find out more
about its auctions, visit its Web site (www.
itsonlyrocknroll.com).

Other photos came from the collection of Steve Pimper, a
picture-sleeve fanatic who has been contributing to KP Books
records price guides for many years. Still others came from
the collections of the author and other KP employees.

INDEX

Abbey Road 11, 15, 19, 27, 31, 272, 295-296, 418-418, 447

"Across the Universe"........................ 98

"Act Naturally" 99, 246-247, 416

"Ain't She Sweet"................ 99, 250, 274

All My Loving 101-102, 255, 259, 413

All Our Loving.............................. 275

"All You Need Is Love"................. 9, 20, 24, 103, 110, 406

Amazing Beatles and Other Great English Group Sounds, The......... 275

American Tour with Ed Rudy, The................................. 275

"And I Love Her"....... 106, 264, 414, 444

"Anna" 109, 267, 413

Anthology 1 .... 1, 276, 447

Anthology 2.............................. 2, 277

Anthology 2 Sampler...................... 277

Anthology 3.............................. 278

"Ask Me Why" 16, 109-110, 207, 267-269, 271, 334-338, 349, 409, 413

Autographs................................ 35, 37-38

Baby It's You 249, 449

"Baby, You're a Rich Man" 20, 25, 103, 105, 110, 406

"Baby's in Black".................... 241, 413

Backbeat................................. 250

"Ballad of John and Yoko, The"..................................110-113

Banks – see Yellow Submarine banks 86

"Be-Bop-a-Lula".................... 113

Beatle Talk 279

Beatlemania Tour Coverage............ 279

Beatles, The........................ 5, 296, 445

Beatles (No. 1), The.................. 6, 413

Beatles Again, The – see Hey Jude.............................. 326

Beatles and Frank Ifield on Stage, The 284

Beatles at the Hollywood Bowl, The 285

Beatles – Circa 1960 – In the Beginning with Tony Sheridan, The 285

Beatles Collection, The 285

Beatles Collection Platinum Series, The 286

Beatles Deluxe Box Set, The 286

Beatles for Sale (LP) 286, 413, 420

Beatles for Sale No. 2 413

Beatles 1962-1966, The 287-288

Beatles 1967-1970, The 289

Beatles 1 6

Beatles VI 290

Beatles '65 .... 71, 294-296

Beatles Special Limited Edition, The 295

Beatles Talk with Jerry G., The 295

Beatles Talk with Jerry G., Vol. 2, The 295

Beatles 10th Anniversary Box Set, The 296

Beatles vs. the Four Seasons, The 297-298

Beatles with Tony Sheridan and Their Guests 298

Beatles' Christmas Album, The 299

Beatles' First Live Recordings, Volume 1, The 300

Beatles' First Live Recordings, Volume 2, The 300

Beatles' Hits, The 413

Beatles' Million Sellers, The 414

"Beatles' Movie Medley, The" 116

Beatles' Second Album, The (EP) 251-252

Beatles' Second Album, The (LP) 301-305

Beatles' Second Open-End Interview, The 253

Beatles' Story, The 306

"Besame Mucho" 227

"Birthday" 116

"Blackbird" 241

Bobb'n Head dolls 39-40

"Boys" 9, 17, 117, 249

British Are Coming, The 307

Bubble bath 41

"Can't Buy Me Love" 17, 118, 406, 414

"Can't Help It 'Blue Angel'" 160

"Christmas Time (Is Here Again)" 121, 131

"Come Together" 16, 31, 226, 409

Comic books 45

Complete Silver Beatles, The 308

Concert posters – see Posters

Concert tickets – see Tickets

"Cry for a Shadow" 122, 242, 250

"Crying, Waiting, Hoping" 122

David Wigg Interviews, The............. 308

Dawn of the Silver Beatles 308

"Day Tripper" 20, 235, 410

"Decade" 16, 28, 122, 431, 448

Disk-Go-Case – see Record cases

"Do You Want to Know a
    Secret" 124-125, 416

"Don't Let Me Down" 133, 407

Drum – see Snare drum

Early Beatles, The 309-310

East Coast Invasion 310

"Eight Days a
    Week"....................20, 128, 404, 413

"Eleanor Rigby" 19-20, 23, 27,
    243, 410

"Everybody's Trying to Be
    My Baby" 229, 257

Extracts from the Album A Hard Day's
    Night..414

Extracts from the Movie A Hard Day's
    Night.......................................311, 392

"Fab Four on Film" 116

"Falling in Love Again".................. 130

First Movement 310

"Flip Your Wig" game 51

"For You Blue"................................ 177

Four by the Beatles 255

4-By the Beatles 257

"Free as a Bird"................131, 448-449

From Britain with Beat! 310

"From Me to You"............. 16, 132, 209,
    406, 413

"German Medley"............................ 133

"Get Back" 27, 31, 133, 135, 407, 424

"Girl" 16, 62, 124, 132,
    135-136, 223, 251, 253, 406, 413

Golden Beatles 310

"Good Day Sunshine" 154

"Got to Get You Into My Life" 30,
    137, 153, 448-449, 463

Great American Tour – 1965 Live
    Beatlemania Concert, The 311

Guitars 40, 53, 80, 133

Hair spray 54

"Hallelujah I Love Her So" 113

Halloween costume 55

"Happy Christmas 1969"................139

"Hard Day's Night, A".............311-314

Hard Day's Night, A..................141-145

Harmonica...56

Hear the Beatles Tell All 314

"Hello Goodbye" 20, 22, 25, 145,
147, 407

"Help!" 17, 20,
70, 149-150, 152, 160, 218, 286, 296,
318, 375-379, 392, 407, 423, 464, 477

"Helter Skelter" 9, 31, 137, 153, 363

"Here, There and Everywhere" 9,
30, 154, 323

"Here Comes the Sun" 154, 187

"Hey
Jude" 27, 155, 157, 283, 295-296,
324, 326-328, 407, 447, 459-460, 472

"Hippy Hippy Shake".......................158

Historic First Live Recordings, The .. 328

"How'd You Get to Know
Her Name"....................................158

"I Am the Walrus"..............25, 145-146,
407, 415

I Apologize 329

"I Don't Know Why I Do
(I Just Do)"...................................168

"I Don't Want to Spoil the
Party"....................................128, 413

"I Feel Fine"................ 17, 52, 158, 404,
408, 414

"I Remember You" 180

"I Saw Her Standing
There".................16, 19, 27,
160-161, 349, 358-359, 413

"I Should Have Known
Better"...................................143, 414

"I Want to Hold Your Hand"....... 16, 19,
27, 160-161, 164, 262, 356,
358-359, 408, 414, 454

"I'll Cry Instead" 165, 264, 311,
313, 414

"I'll Get You" 167, 219, 224, 409

"I'll Have Everything Too"..............168

"I'll Try Anyway" 168, 243

"I'm Checking Out Now Baby"........168

"I'm Down" 150, 407

"I'm Gonna Sit Right Down and Cry
Over You"....................................168

"I'm Happy Just to Dance
with You"..............................116, 165

"I've Just Seen a Face" 248

"If I Fell"...........................106, 264, 414

"If I Needed Someone"....................195

"If You Can't Get Her".....................158

"If You Love Me Baby" 177

Introducing the Beatles........5, 296-297, 330, 333, 339, 343, 363, 388-389

"It's All Too Much" 169

Jolly What! The Beatles and Frank Ifield on Stage.................................284, 344

"Julia"...199

"Kansas City".....................................117

"Kansas City-Hey Hey Hey Hey".......169

"Lady Madonna" 27, 31, 170, 408, 454

Lamp 60

"Leave My Kitten Alone" 174

"Lend Me Your Comb" 174

"Let It Be" 11, 27, 32, 70, 123, 135, 175, 296, 346, 390, 408, 424, 446

"Let's Dance" 177

Lightning Strikes Twice 348

"Like Dreamers Do" 177, 348

"Little Queenie"................................230

Live, 1962, Hamburg, Germany 349

Live at the BBC 349, 446-447, 449

Live at the Star Club in Hamburg, Germany, 1962 350

"Long and Winding Road, The"177-179

"Long Tall Sally" 180, 251, 302, 305, 414

"Love Me Do"..........................15-16, 56, 180-184, 330-333, 362, 409, 413, 449

"Love of the Loved" 177, 187

Love Songs 23, 350, 447

"Lucy in the Sky with Diamonds".........................30-31, 187

Lunchbox – see Yellow Submarine lunchbox

"Magical Mystery Tour".....25, 187-188, 295-296, 351, 382, 411, 415, 468

Magical Mystery Tour (EP) 415

"Matchbox"......189, 215, 225, 264, 414

Meet the Beatles! (EP) 259

Meet the Beatles! (LP) 355-361

"Memphis"...187

Merry Christmas and Happy New Year 239, 271

"Misery".........................216, 267, 413

"Mr. Moonlight" 240, 257

"More Than I Need Myself" 223

Movie posters – see Posters

Moviemania 361

"Music City/KFWBeatles" 191

"My Bonnie" 16, 250

"1964: Season's Greetings from the Beatles".. 193

1965 Talk Album – Ed Rudy with New U.S. Tour...................................... 361

"1966: Season's Greetings from the Beatles"................................. 130, 194

"Nobody's Child" 99

"Norwegian Wood (This Bird Has Flown)".. 195

Not a Second Time 361

"Nowhere Man" 29, 196, 416

"Ob-La-Di, Ob-La-Da" 174, 199, 463

"Octopus's Garden" 154

Oil paint sets...........................65-66

"Old Brown Shoe" 110, 406

"Only a Northern Song" 169

Open-End Interview with the Beatles 262, 279, 392

Original Greatest Hits, The.............. 362

"P.S. I Love You" 16, 181, 330-333, 409, 413

"Paperback Writer" 20, 22-23, 200, 409

Past Masters Volume 1 and 2.......... 362

"Penny Lane" 20, 23, 95, 202-204, 227, 409

"Please Please Me" 10, 16, 37, 56, 207, 209, 334-338, 362, 409, 413, 425, 477

Portraits 63, 69

Posters...........................8, 33, 47-48, 70

Puzzles – see Yellow Submarine puzzles

"Rain"..........................20, 23, 200, 409

Rarities............9, 11, 285, 308, 362, 477

"Real Love".....................214, 448-449

Record cases 76-77

Record player.............................. 14, 78

Recorded Live in Hamburg, Vol. 1 .... 110, 113, 130, 158, 160, 168-169, 174, 180, 215, 227, 229-230, 240, 300, 363

Recorded Live in Hamburg, Vol. 2 .... 110, 113, 130, 158, 160, 168-169, 174, 180, 215, 227, 229-230, 240, 300, 363

Recorded Live in Hamburg, Vol. 3 .... 110, 113, 130, 158, 160, 168-169, 174, 180, 215, 227, 229-230, 240, 300, 363

"Red Sails in the Sunset"................. 215

Reel Music.............................363, 443

"Revolution"......................27, 155, 407

Revolver 19, 23, 29, 295-296,
364, 427, 471, 477

"Rock and Roll Music" 122, 413

Rock 'n' Roll Music 368, 446-447,
451

Rock 'n' Roll Music, Volume 1 368

Rock 'n' Roll Music, Volume 2 368

"Rocky Raccoon" 215

"Roll Over Beethoven" 168,
216-217, 253, 255

Round the World 368

Rubber Soul.....................19, 23, 28-29,
295-296, 369, 427, 477

"Ruby Baby"....................................218

Savage Young Beatles, The.............374

Sgt. Pepper's Lonely Hearts Club
Band....................19, 23, 330, 36, 72,
295-296, 375, 381-382, 417, 428, 464

"She Loves You"...........8, 14, 16, 19, 27,
167, 219-220, 224-225, 405, 409, 414

"She's a Woman".............158, 404, 408

"She's Not the Only Girl
in Town".....................................223

"Sheila" 130, 350

"Shimmy Shake"............................227

"Sie Liebt Dich (She Loves
You)"...................................224-225

Silver Beatles, The 383

Silver Beatles, Volume 1 383

Silver Beatles, Volume 2 383

"Slow Down" 189-190, 225, 264, 414

Snare drum......................................80

"Something"...................11, 14, 16-17,
25, 27-28, 226, 264, 295-296, 339,
384, 409, 434-435, 440-441, 443

Something New (EP).................264-266

Something New (LP) 384-387

Songs and Pictures of the Fabulous
Beatles...387

Songs, Pictures and Stories of the
Fabulous Beatles 388

Souvenir of Their Visit to America... 267

"Strawberry Fields Forever".........19-20,
23-24, 27, 95, 202, 206, 227, 409

"Sweet Georgia Brown"......99, 227, 240

"Sweet Little Sixteen".......................158

"Take Good Care of My Baby" 122

"Take Out Some Insurance on Me
Baby"..227

Talcum powder 4, 81

Talk Downunder 390

"Talkin' Bout You" 227

"Taste of Honey, A" 227

"Taxman" 30. 116

"Thank You Girl" 16, 124, 132, 251, 253, 406, 413

"There's a Place" 231, 363, 416

"Things We Said Today" 145, 390, 407, 414

"This Boy" 101, 164, 255, 259, 262, 311-312, 408

This Is Where It Started 390

"Three Cool Cats" 177, 229

Three-ring binders 82

"Ticket to Ride" 17, 228, 410

Tickets 33, 46, 83-84, 285

"Till There Was You" 229, 350, 358, 360

Timeless 390

Timeless II 390

"To Know Her Is to Love Her" 230

20 Greatest Hits 391, 447

20 Hits, Beatles 392

"Twist and Shout" 110, 230-231, 337, 349, 404, 416, 466

Twist and Shout 110, 230-231, 337, 349, 404, 416, 466

"Two of Us" 98

"We Can Work It Out" 235, 410

We Wish You a Merry Christmas and a Happy New Year 239

West Coast Invasion 392

"What Goes On" 196

"What'd I Say" 240

"When I'm 64" 187

"Where Have You Been All My Life" 240, 350

"While My Guitar Gently Weeps" 241

White Album, The – See Beatles, The

"Why" 3, 7-9, 11, 13-16, 27, 36, 38-43, 56, 109-110, 168, 207, 215, 242-243, 264, 267-269, 271, 334-338, 349, 409, 413-414

"Why Don't We Do It in the Road?" 215

With the Beatles 33, 43, 54, 208, 262, 393, 429, 477

WLS chart 10

"WMCA Good Guys" 164

Wristwatch 85

"Ya Ya" 218

"Yellow Submarine".............. 23, 30, 33, 70, 85-94, 243, 296, 394, 396, 410, 430, 447

Yellow Submarine................. 23, 30, 33, 70, 85-94, 243, 296, 394, 396, 410, 430, 447

Yellow Submarine banks.................... 86

Yellow Submarine lunchbox............. 90

Yellow Submarine puzzles................. 92

"Yes It Is"................................228, 410

"Yesterday"........................... 20, 99, 246, 296, 391-392, 397, 404, 416, 449

Yesterday 20, 99, 246, 296, 391-392, 397, 404, 416, 449

Yesterday and Today................ 296, 397

"You Can't Do That" 118, 191, 319, 322, 406

"You Know My Name (Look Up My Number)" 175, 408

"You're Going to Lose That Girl"..... 136

"Your Feets Too Big" 174

"You've Got to Hide Your Love Away".......................... 102, 248